STO

**DO NOT REMOVE
CARDS FROM POCKET**

1/20/94

50 Things You Can Do to Save American Jobs

Gregory Matusky
and
David R. Evanson

A CITADEL PRESS BOOK
Published by Carol Publishing Group

A Citadel Press Book
Published by Carol Publishing Group

Citadel Press is a registered trademark of Carol Communications, Inc.
Editorial Offices: 600 Madison Avenue, New York, N.Y. 10022
Sales & Distribution Offices: 120 Enterprise Avenue, Secaucus, N.J. 07094
In Canada: Canadian Manda Group, P.O. Box 920, Station U, Toronto,
    Ontario M8Z 5P9
Queries regarding rights and permissions should be addressed to
Carol Publishing Group, 600 Madison Avenue, New York, N.Y. 10022

Carol Publishing Group books are available at special discounts
for bulk purchases, for sales promotions, fund-raising, or
educational purposes. Special editions can be created to specifications.
For details contact: Special Sales Department, Carol Publishing
Group, 120 Enterprise Avenue, Secaucus, N.J. 07094

Manufactured in the United States of America

10 9 8 7 6 5 4 3 2 1

Library of Congress Cataloging-in-Publication Data

Matusky, Gregory, 1961–
    50 things you can do to save American jobs / by Gregory Matusky and
David R. Evanson.
        p.   cm
    "A Citadel Press book."
    ISBN 0–8065–1414–0 (pbk.)
    1. Foreign trade and employment—United States.   2. Unemployment—
United States.   3. Buy national policy—United States.
I. Evanson, David R., 1959– . II. Title. III. Title: Fifty things
you can do to save American jobs.
HD5710.75.U6M37   1993
331.13′77′0973—dc20   92–38090
                                                                  CIP

Dedication

To my wife, Judy, without whom nothing would be worthwhile. To Jonathan, Megan, and Jessica, who sacrificed time
with their father so this book could be written. To Paul
Matusky, my father, who is living testimony to the
posssibilities that are America and who played gofer while I
wrote.

Gregory Matusky

To my father Stanley Evanson, to my children, David and
Madeline, and, most devotedly, to my wife, Perri, without
whose love and support this project would not have been
completed.

David R. Evanson

Finally, to all Americans who might be searching for a job.
Your plight is what inspired this work and gave us the
fortitude to see it through to completion. May you all find
jobs and opportunities due to the fifty things outlined here.

The Authors

Contents

Acknowledgments

We owe a debt of gratitude to many people who gave freely of their time, advice, and resources. You'll see many of them mentioned in this book among the various case studies and interviews. But there are also many who are not mentioned. First among these are our dedicated researchers, Donna Cavanagh, Beth D'Addono, and Virginia Simon, who always met our impossible deadlines with good cheer and good work; Denise Marcil, without whom the book never would have happened; Echo Garrett, who motivated us to go forward in the darkest moment of this project; and Tony DeFazio and Renee Carey, dedicated staffers of Gregory Communications, Inc., who held down the fort while this book was being written.

Foreword

The idea for this book originated one evening twelve months ago during the depths of the recession. At the time, all three major networks ended their nightly newscasts with heart-wrenching stories of unemployed Americans. Before the television set played two young children, who begged the question: Would they grow up to enjoy the same opportunities as their fathers had enjoyed? That defining moment launched a quest to find the fifty steps any American could take to create or preserve jobs in this country.

Since then, the outlook for American jobs has not improved. As we put the finishing touches on this book, Sears announced a massive layoff of 50,000 employees. In the same week, United Technologies, Boeing, and Eastman Kodak reported severe cutbacks.

The fallout of these layoffs is devastating in both economic and human terms. When jobs go, so do homes, cars, funds for college educations, self-esteems, and marriages. But the biggest victims of this economic devastation is our own dreams. The American Dream is turning into a nightmare for those witnessing the unraveling of their own economic well-being. Jobs—the fiber of our economic future—are being pulled out from beneath us.

But it doesn't have to be this way. Each of us can make a difference. We have the power to end the erosion and put Americans back to work. Some steps require education. Others demand a change in the way we buy products and services. Still others require that we adjust our attitudes to meet the challenges of a global economy.

You can't do every single thing in this book. But then, the task of saving American jobs is not yours alone. Your obligation is to do what you can, and to do it faithfully. Let this book serve as your guide.

Things You Need to Know to Save American Jobs

1

The Ten Commandments of Creating Jobs

*More of us could generate jobs for friends and family by
following these ten simple rules.*

1. Look at labels. It sounds trite. But once you start reading
the labels, you'll learn that there are plenty of American-made
products that meet or beat imports. The label should serve as
your first point of reference for buying any product.

2. Seek out training wherever and whenever possible. In the
new employment world order, education will become the pass-
port to opportunity and advancement. In the coming decade,
American workers will change jobs and careers at unprecedented rates six or more times before they retire. Those who
survive the card shuffling will be those who continually
upgrade their skills to cover just about any eventuality.

3. Embrace productivity. To compete against workers in
Dublin or Dubai, we need to increase our productivity as
workers. In short, that means doing more with less, creating
new products with less input, generating more information
with fewer workers. We need to encourage unions, managers,
and colleagues to think smart and work smart and to invest in
the plant and equipment we need to produce higher-quality
products more quickly.

**4. Retaliate where necessary; ingratiate where pos-
sible.** Unbridled free trade is a thing of the past. By throwing
open our markets to countries that fail to open their markets to
American products and businesses, we lower our own standards of living by exporting jobs overseas. We need to embrace

3

those countries that prove themselves to be trade partners and retaliate against those that are nothing more than trade parasites.

5. Challenge foreign countries to meet our environmental and social standards before buying their products. It's easy for Mexico to undercut the price of American-made products when it spews deadly fumes into the air and forces workers to live in squalor. It's easy for China to grab an increasing share of the American market when the costs of its products are subsidized by prison labor. Americans must refuse to buy these countries' products.

6. Realize that the environment and job creation can go hand-in-hand. Recycling creates jobs and puts Americans to work. The pollution control industry represents one of this country's greatest opportunities to generate new jobs in the future. By tying the environment to job creation, we build a powerful alliance that's sure to make a difference.

7. Savings is a key to saving jobs. We must increase our personal savings rate if we are to have the money needed to create jobs. Businesses need money to build the plants and buy the equipment needed to put people to work. When we save—through stocks, bonds, or savings accounts—we are pouring money into the economy to put people to work.

8. Teach our children well. It's time to shake up American education. Our children desperately need the sophisticated skills required to survive and thrive in a high-tech economy. Parents must take an active role in making sure their children are being challenged in the classroom so that they can meet the challenges of the world of work.

9. Sound-off. We need to voice our opinions to elected officials, business leaders, and each other. We need to encourage, object, and make noise when we see initiatives that steal jobs from hardworking Americans. We need to write letters, use the telephone, and meet face-to-face with those who threaten the foundation of our country—jobs.

10. Pull together. We must realize that the overwhelming challenge of the 1990s and beyond is to retain our standard of living so that the progress we have made as a society won't

erode due to poverty and unemployment. All of us—environ-
mentalists, legislators, manufacturers, managers, union heads,
educators, parents, and workers—must come to the same
realization: that without jobs America becomes a Third World
nation, dashing the hopes of all of us.

2

Seven Myths About America's Job Problems

American workers, products, and companies
have been falsely ridiculed here and abroad.
By telling the true story, we can create stronger
demand for our products and more jobs for our people.

OVERVIEW

We have seen the handwringing. We have heard the ruminations: Americans are lazy. Americans can't make things. Americans don't work hard. America is a second-class economic power.

Well, it just isn't so. Much of what you have been hearing from Americans—about American productivity and America's inability to compete—isn't the truth. It's not so much that we've been deceived, it's that we are our own toughest critics. We look for problems and then often exaggerate them when we find them.

Since economics is fueled by attitudes, opinions, and yes, exaggerations, this self-criticism can be dangerous. If everyone believes our economy is in decline, then it becomes a self-fulfilling prophecy. And when decline sets in, jobs and opportunities disappear.

The surest and simplest step Americans can take to save U.S. jobs is to arm themselves with the facts.

Seven Myths We Want to Change

1. Americans Are Lazy and Unproductive. Not true. By many measures Americans are the most productive workers on the face of the earth. According to the Organization for Economic Cooperation and Development in a study released in 1992, the average American worker added roughly $21,450 in output to the U.S. domestic product. The average West German contributed $18,559 and the average Japanese added only $17,490. What do these figures mean? Simply that the average American worker produces more value than his foreign counterparts. And that's what productivity is all about. As for the "lazy" label, while most American workers keep their vacations to two weeks, French and German workers take off entire months during the summer to enjoy a holiday.

2. Americans Can't Build the Products the World Wants. Simply ridiculous. The United States is the world's leading exporter, selling more than $388 billion worth of products and $148 billion worth of services overseas each year. And we design, develop, and manufacturer many of the world's most sought-after products. Need proof? Look to Gillette Co., which sells more than $500 million worth of razors and blades each year. It commands nearly 70 percent of Europe's market for wet razors and 80 percent of Latin America's. The company has gone toe-to-toe with foreign competitors, including Wilkenson-Sword in the 1970s, whose blade business Gillette now owns, and Bic (disposable razors) in the 1980s. Both times, Gillette rose to the challenge by introducing higher-quality products that won shavers' loyalties.

3. America Needs to Become More Like Japan. Granted, Japan's way of doing business is more conducive to some aspects of business. But are Americans willing to sacrifice their individualism and sense of self in order to match Japan? Japan's success has, to a large extent, been based on minimizing the role of the individual for the good of the team or group. Americans returning from Japan know all too well the Japanese proverb "Live life as if you are dead." Translation: check out your individualism when you check into Japan. But individual initiative accounts for many of America's greatest gifts to the world, including Edison's discovery of the light bulb and Bill Gates' worldwide triumph with DOS, the top-selling computer language. America needs to change if it's to win in the new global economy. But Japan may not be the role model.

4. Americans Can't Work Together to Tackle Problems.
Throughout our history, America's greatest strength has been our predilection to join together to meet challenges. The Gulf War proved that point. Our great diversity gives us a rich, lush gene pool to call upon for new ideas and initiatives. The variety of our people and their heritage is not a disadvantage—it is something we must lean on to solve the economic problems we now face.

5. Americans Can't Compete in the Sciences. How do you explain the creative dominance of Americans in the field of biotechnology? Americans have displayed unprecedented know-how in this field, and our achievements include advancements in pharmaceuticals, early cancer detection, genetically-altered vegetables that are more insect-resistant, and the use of bacteria to help control pollution or extract oils from plants to use as fuel. Basic research at American colleges and universities, as well as in public and private U.S. laboratories, is the best in the world.

6. American Products Are Second-Rate. Except for the notable exceptions that always haunt us, mainly automobiles and consumer electronics, America leads the world in industries as diverse as aircraft building and motorcycle manufacturing. Need evidence? With worldwide sales of more than $28 billion in 1990, Boeing Company in Seattle markets its products in just about every country the law allows. Boeing is our country's largest net exporter, accounting for 7.2 percent of U.S. capital goods exports in 1990. And how about Harley-Davidson, Inc.? Harley hogs are the most sought-after muscle bikes in the world. At last word the company had sold out its 1993 orders. About one in every three Harleys is sold overseas.

7. The American Economy Is Now Second to Japan's. Get a grip. Our GNP was $5.68 trillion in 1992. That's about double the size of Japan's. Granted, Japan has only half the population. But make no mistake, we're still an economic superpower, by just about any measure.

3

Spreading the Word

Word of mouth is the single most effective way
for Americans to help save jobs.

OVERVIEW

Every businessperson knows that the best way to market a product is through word of mouth.

The same goes for saving American jobs. During the 1970s and 1980s, the word on the street when it came to many American products was bad. And with good reason: the quality simply wasn't there. In autos. In consumer electronics. In computers. In scores of other products. And we were more than happy to tell ourselves so.

A compelling example was the Bannister family of Blue Hill, Maine. In the 1980s, they were featured on a Honda commercial trumpeting the fact that they had bought nothing but Hondas during the past decade.

But now guess what? The Bannisters are driving Dodge minivans, and Dodge was smart enough to put them in its commercials to explain why they switched from imports to American-made cars.

We need more of the Bannisters of the world to give American products another try. When they do, they're bound to discover that the quality of American products has improved dramatically over the past five years.

What You Can Do

Spread the word. Nothing is more influential than a personal endorsement, especially when the word comes from someone who uses a product or service.

But how can you persuade a relative or friend to buy American without seeming like a salesperson or offending whoever you're talking to? While researching, we faced that challenge repeatedly. We were told by an accountant to forget the buy-American plea, since consumers are only interested in getting the lowest possible price for any product. We were also told that most Americans won't listen to the message, because they simply don't care.

But then we learned some lessons in how to deliver the message. We distilled them into five easy-to-follow rules:

1. *Don't preach.* No one likes preaching. If you harp on a subject, people stop listening. Sermonizing will only leave you friendless.

2. *Practice what you preach* (although preaching isn't allowed). The world is full of great American products that can compete with any on the face of the earth. Make it a habit to buy these products as much as possible. You don't have to be a purist; a global economy assures that you will own foreign-made products. But the more you commit to saving American jobs through your buying habits, the more weight you'll carry when trying to persuade others to join the cause.

3. *Know your stuff.* Before you champion a cause, do some research, find out the facts, then make it part of your message. You don't have to be a walking encyclopedia. But if you know that an American car has won three industry awards, spreading the word could lead a friend or neighbor to the showroom.

4. *Relate things to people's lives.* When we first started discussing this book with friends and neighbors, we took a much higher line of debate. The global economy, we argued, had not worked as we had assumed it would. Instead of lifting American affluence by building overseas markets for our products, it had actually lowered the American standard of living, by forcing us to compete against poverty-wage workers. And from that, we got a big, and well-deserved, yawn.

The concepts were too detached from people's lives. So instead, we started asking people a simple question: "What happens to your job when everyone stops buying the products or services that your company sells?" That made the point and won us followers.

5. *Believe in what you are saying.* We can, as Americans, do the little things needed to bring jobs and opportunity back to this country. It doesn't take an economist or the government to make a difference. We can make differences by buying the right products, voting for the right people, supporting the right causes, and improving ourselves and the country we live in. But we have to believe in the importance of individual initiative if we are to safeguard the American standard of living and provide our children the same opportunities we have enjoyed.

Sources

How to Get Your Point Across in 30 Seconds or Less. Milo O. Frank. Simon & Schuster, New York.

How to Make Friends and Influence People. Dale Carnegie. Simon & Schuster, New York.

Influence Without Authority. Allan R. Cohen and David Bradford. John Wiley & Sons, Inc., New York.

Persuasion: A Means of Social Influence. Winston L. Brembeck and William S. Howell. Prentice-Hall, Inc., Englewood Cliffs, New Jersey.

4

Magnify Your Political Clout a Hundredfold

It's not just on Election Day that you can send a message to politicians. You can do it every day of the year, and leverage your impact in the process.

OVERVIEW

As a consumer, you vote every day with your dollars. As a constituent, you may think your influence is limited to one day a year: Election Day. But this is simply not true! You can have an impact on Capitol Hill any day of the week simply by writing a letter. *Write your Congressman.* Sounds trite, doesn't it? But listen to this. "The rule of thumb used by politicians," says Stephen Young of 20/20 Vision, a nonprofit organization in Washington, D.C., dedicated to more effective lobbying techniques, "is that every letter received represents one hundred constituents. Studies have shown that writing a letter is the single most effective lobbying effort any citizen can make."

Why? Because too many times, important elections could have gone the other way if just one person in every precinct had voted the other way. Politicians understand this. They know the numbers game. So when your letter comes in, representing as it does the opinion of a hundred other constituents, you can bet that ears start to perk up. People who have been on the inside of the political machinery will readily back this up. Barbara Shaffer, a legislative assistant to former New Jersey Congressman Frank Guarini, says, "We took a close look at every single letter that came into the office. If we received ten letters on one issue [read 1,000 constituents], that carried a lot of weight.

12

Letters are so important to politicians that in almost every office it's someone's full-time job to read the mail." Another legislative aide sums it up this way: "If a voter takes the time to write a letter, it gets read."

Here's how it all adds up. You don't have to be an expert. You don't have to be a good writer. You just have to have a stamp, a pen, some paper, and an opinion to magnify your political clout a hundredfold.

What You Can Do

Start writing for American jobs. It's easy. If you have an opinion about what the state and federal governments should be doing to create and/or safeguard American jobs, write it down and send it to your state and federal representatives. If there is legislation pending that you feel will create or destroy American jobs, write your thoughts down about that, too, and send it off.

Here are ten more issues worth writing to your elected representatives about.

- Write to your elected representatives and tell them that you believe it is important to encourage industry to keep jobs here in the United States. The reason: shipping jobs overseas benefits few and hurts many.

- Write to your elected representatives and tell them that you believe it is important to support defense conversion. The reason: as the defense budget shrinks, it's essential that we help our defense contractors find commercial and civilian markets for their products and services.

- Write to your elected representatives and tell them that you believe it is important to crack down on abusers of American free trade practices. The reason: they steal American jobs and undermine the fiber of the free enterprise system.

- Write to your elected representatives and tell them that you believe it is important to encourage investment in biotechnology. The reason: worldwide revenues are expected to grow from the current $4 billion, of which $3 billion a year is in the United States, to more than $60 billion by the year 2000.

• Write to your elected representatives and tell them that you believe it is important to make improvements to our infrastructure. The reason: building and improving roads, bridges, and ports puts Americans to work, and enhances the collective productivity and competitiveness of American industry.

• Write to your elected representatives and tell them that you believe it is important to contain health care costs. The reason: skyrocketing medical and insurance costs divert capital from investment in the property, plants, and equipment that create jobs. Moreover, containment of these costs diverts management time away from the more important task of improving quality and productivity.

• Write to your elected representatives and tell them that you believe it is important to adopt a national energy policy. The reason: without one there is no strategy for reducing our dependence on foreign oil, a major source of trade imbalance and a drain on American jobs.

• Write to your elected representatives and tell them that you believe it is important to encourage investment in environmental technologies. The reason: the resulting products and services put Americans to work in an emerging industry, and these cleansing technologies will leave our children a better world.

• Write to your elected representatives and tell them that you believe it is important to assist in technology transfer. The reason: while the American basic research enterprise is the envy of the world, our track record of transforming discoveries into important new products is not. Fax and VCR technologies are just two sad examples in a long list of missed opportunities.

Here's How to Write a Better Letter

Legislative aides told us what makes a letter effective. In summary:

- Don't write to a representative outside of your district. You have almost no clout there.

- Be specific in the first paragraph about the purpose of your letter.

- Unless you are an expert, or are offering new information, keep your letter to one page.

- Send a copy of the letter to the newspapers in the representatives' districts and let them know you did this. "That will definitely get their attention," aides say.

- Don't vent spleen. This only obscures your communication.

- Try to tie the issue that you are writing about to your own experiences (e.g., "We now buy savings bonds with the money we saved on taxes . . .") or an event you may have witnessed.

Here's How to Find Your Representatives

Look in the blue pages of your telephone book or check your local post office—it probably posts the names and addresses of your federal representatives on a bulletin board. If it does not, ask the postmaster if a list is handy. If you really get serious, Contact Software International, Carroll, Texas, has developed a user-friendly program called *Write Your Congressman* that is available for DOS systems. For $49 you get a current data base of congressmen and -women, with a template of model letters. The program makes writing and addressing letters a snap. Call 214-919-9500 for more information.

5

Using Your Library

*In order to safeguard American jobs, you have
to have the facts.*

OVERVIEW

The great physicist Albert Einstein did not even know his own phone number. "Why should I?" he asked. "True knowledge is not knowing the facts, but knowing where to find them." You can find almost all the facts you need to help you safeguard American jobs at your local library. All totaled, there are 116,216 libraries in the United States. And most are staffed with trained professionals to help you find the information you're looking for. Many of us would buy American products, or avoid products from certain countries, or support politicians with a track record of creating jobs, if only we knew the facts. If a friend was out of work, would you spend three hours helping him or her find a job? Of course you would. Why not do the same thing for your country? By investing those same three hours in your local library, you can save a job. You can create a job. By diligently applying what you learn over the course of a lifetime, who knows how many jobs you can create? Read on to find out the kind of essential information you can pick up in just a single tour of a nearby library.

Corporate Ownership. Forget saving American jobs for the moment. Isn't it just good, common sense to know something about the companies whose products you use every day? When you go to the library, think about the many products you use and consume regularly—things like cosmetics, pens, umbrellas, auto parts, and pasta. Then look up the companies that manufacture these products. Finding out a little bit more about them is fun. It's also very easy. Here are four directories that can tell you whether or not the companies that make your favorite products are American companies.

- *The International Directory of Corporate Affiliations.* This invaluable book is subtitled *Who Owns Whom: The Family Tree of Every Major Corporation.* Parents, subsidiaries, and divisions are cross-referenced. For the parent company, ownership information as well as location is provided. National Register Publishing, Macmillan, Inc. Wilmette, Illinois.
- *Hoover Handbook of World Businesses.* In this guide, which is referenced by company name, you can find general company, sales, and geographical information, plus a brief history. There is also a companion American company version of this publication. The Reference Press, Austin, Texas.
- *Million Dollar Directory.* Offers current sales, credit, geographical, and in many cases, ownership information. Dun & Bradstreet, Inc., Parsippany, New Jersey.
- *Trade Names Directory.* With this directory, you can look up products by the brand name to find its manufacturer. For example, Crest will yield Procter & Gamble, the behemoth consumer products company located in Cincinnati. Gale Research, Inc., Detroit, Michigan.

Foreign Countries. We're not chanting "Buy American" like a mantra. Foreign trade is good. It opens markets abroad for American products. And the foreign products in our country urge domestic manufacturers on to even higher levels of excellence and service. But these benefits occur only when the playing field between trading partners is a level one. So when you buy foreign, buy from our partners, not from our parasites. How can you learn more about other countries and foreign trade issues? Here's three good sources easily found in almost any library.

- *The Statesman's Yearbook.* Organized by country, this publication provides information about the constitution, government, climate, diplomatic representatives, and commerce of almost every foreign nation on the face of the earth. A brief history is also provided. St. Martin's Press, New York, New York.

- *The Pacific Rim Almanac.* First of all, what is the Pacific Rim? It consists of the established and emerging economies on the rim of the Asian continent, including Japan, Korea, Taiwan, Malaysia, and Indonesia. This almanac will tell you about these countries that are flooding the American market with their goods. Better yet, using the almanac's ample supply of facts and statistics can help you decide which countries' products to avoid. HarperPerennial, a division of Harper-Collins Publishing, New York, New York.
- *Congressional Quarterly Weekly Report.* There's so much information here, it's a little intimidating. Start by looking up foreign trade in the index. Then turn to the page and find out what foreign trade issues our elected officials are talking about. Congressional Quarterly, Inc., Washington, D.C.

Politicians. You can vote for American jobs every election day, by putting men and women in office who stand up for American workers and American jobs. Part of this means paying attention, and perhaps reading between the lines of political rhetoric. But you also need to know where our politicians stand on the issues, and how they have voted in the past. You can do this easily at your library by using any of the following publications.

- *The Almanac of American Politics.* Among other things, this fascinating compendium lumps together votes by topic so you can see who voted how on things like education, foreign trade, and manufacturing outreach programs. National Journal, Washington, D.C.
- *CQ Almanac.* Find out not only how your politicians voted, but also read some of the essays and commentaries to understand the issues being debated. CQ Inc., Washington, D.C.

And remember, it's not just knowing about the politicians that makes you a better consumer, it's also learning about the mechanics of government. By doing so, you know who to call to ask further questions, or to report suspicions or unfair trade practices. For this purpose, two books are invaluable.

- *The United States Government Manual.* The bulk—and we mean bulk—of this manual lists organizations, committees, agencies, and quasi-official agencies of the legislative, judicial, and executive branches of the federal government. Bernan Press, Lanham, Maryland.
- *Information U.S.A.* You'll find lots of information on the United States government organized by department. For example, at the U.S. International Trade Commission, you can find out who is in charge of everything from acetone to zippers, as well as their address and telephone number. Viking Penguin Books, New York, New York.

Product Information. To find out more about some of the best *American*-made products, ask the reference librarian if the library subscribes to: *Consumer Reports, Consumer Guide, Consumer Digest,* or *Consumer Research.*

Sources

Sometimes, your need for information outstrips the resources of your library. When this happens remember that trade associations are a great source of additional information, and that there is an association for just about any cause, product, or group that you can imagine. Still, your library can get you going in the right direction when you are looking for a trade association. Look for *The Encyclopedia of Associations,* published by Gale Research, Inc., or *National and Professional Associations of the United States,* published by Columbia Books.

6

Let Your Fingers Do the Squawking

When you are given a voice, by all means, use it!

OVERVIEW

You can save American jobs just by using your voice. That's right. The American companies that make the products and offer the services we use, no matter how large, are surprisingly sensitive to what you say and think. Consider this. In 1991, the latest year for which figures are available, American companies spent more than $126 billion on advertising alone according to *Advertising Age* magazine. That's money spent just to make a favorable impression.

Many companies go even further, actively promoting 800 numbers and encouraging consumers to call and voice their opinions on products and services. According to AT&T, some half a million U.S. businesses use more than 1.3 million 800 numbers, and the use of these toll-free numbers by American companies has doubled since 1983. You might also be interested to know that 800 service is a uniquely American phenomenon invented by AT&T. In Japan, for instance, toll-free calling was just recently introduced.

While here in the United States, many toll-free lines are used for sales orders, reservations, and credit card authorizations, fully 25 percent are used for some form of customer service, including "hot lines," product inquiries, and customer reports and complaints. Many large consumer products companies even put 800 numbers right on their products so that you can

20

call with questions or comments. Getting the picture? Many American companies want you to reach out and touch *them*.

What You Can Do

Start dialing for American jobs. Here are three simple ways: (1) Use these 800 numbers to make yourself a better consumer; (2) Use them to praise and reward companies that implement practices and policies that promote American jobs; and (3) use them to lodge your displeasure with companies that have shipped jobs overseas, or engaged in what you consider unfair (and, dare we say, un-American?) trade practices.

As a Consumer...

What is a "better consumer"? One whose buying habits lead to the creation, not the elimination, of American jobs. Toll-free numbers can help you do this by giving you access to the facts.

Start calling the toll-free numbers on many of the foods, beauty/grooming aides, medicines, and consumer products that you buy. Find out if the company that makes the product is American or foreign-owned. If the company is American, find out where the product you bought was manufactured. Use this information next time you go shopping, and buy the products that help the American economy.

A note of caution. Many of the people you speak to, though well informed, may not immediately know the answer to your question. Be patient. Ask them to call you back after some research. You'll find in most cases that they will, or else give you another telephone number to call.

As a Cheerleader...

You can catch more flies with honey than you can with vinegar, the old saying goes. And this is no less true for corporations than it is for people. Businesses love to hear their praises sung. It validates their planning and strategy, it motivates their employees, and it strengthens their bond to the community. Some savvy companies even leverage the praise they receive by actively publicizing it in the local press.

You can pat almost any company on the back using 800 numbers. And if your praise hits a chord, you can bet it will get delivered to the president's office. Here's six praises you might consider singing.

• Call a company and express your loyalty to it because it manufactures its product here in the United States.

• Call a company and express your gratitude for its efforts to bring its production back into the United States.

• Call a company and express your admiration at its ability to do a better job than its foreign competition.

• Call a company and express your approval of its efforts to train and retrain its workers.

• Call a company and express your admiration for its ability to produce goods at prices similar to those of manufacturers that rely on cheap, and sometimes unfair, foreign wages.

• Call a company and express your pleasure with its policy of highlighting American-made products.

And as a Complainer...

While you can catch more flies with honey, that doesn't mean you can't catch any with vinegar. And let's face it, companies do react to complaints, especially when they get a lot of them at one time. When complaining, you need to be firm, not mean, and you need to package your complaint so that it can be passed along easily, creating maximum effect as it travels up the corporate ladder. If you care about safeguarding American jobs, here are five events you might consider howling about.

• Complain to any company that has lost substantial or majority market share to foreign competition. Let it know that its apparent lack of ingenuity is embarrassing to you.

• Complain to any company that has shipped jobs overseas to gain modest cost advantages. Let it know that labor savings are often illusory, but that the loss to the American economy is not.

• Complain to any company that misleads consumers into believing the product it makes or sells is American when it is not. Tell it that capitalizing on an important issue is shameful.

• Complain to any company that has announced or implemented wholesale layoffs. Let it know you feel it should have tried harder to find a solution.

• Complain to any company that does not carry many American products in its inventory or on its shelves. Let it know that you prefer to do business with those that do.

Leveraging Your Praise and Your Wrath

In corporate America, it doesn't take too many calls for an "important trendline" to start emerging in the minds of management. You can leverage your impact by having others call. The availability of a toll-free number will increase their willingness to pick up the phone and start dialing for American jobs. So... tell a friend. Ask your relatives to call. Ask your minister to make an announcement in church. Post a note on a community bulletin board. Make photocopies of the toll-free number, along with the complaint or praise, and give it to all your coworkers, or leave a stack next to your automated teller.

Sources

Get an *AT&T Toll-Free 800 Directory*. The consumer directory, which has 60,000 listings, is $9.95, and the business directory, with 120,000 listings, is $14.95. To order call 800-426-8686. Even without the directory, you can still find a lot of toll-free numbers simply by calling 800 information. The number is— you guessed it—800-555-1212.

7

Hiring Illegal Immigrants Can Sap American Jobs

Many people say that illegal immigrants do the work that Americans won't touch. Tell them they're dead wrong.

OVERVIEW

Throughout the industrial age, U.S. immigration policy was come one, come all—the more the better. We were a young nation and we had cities to build, railroads to lay, canals to dig, and prairies to plow. So, the eight million immigrants who landed on America's shores between 1900 and 1910 found plenty of work and a world of opportunity.

Even today, America still lives up to her cultural heritage by accepting legal immigrants from every nation on earth. And we do it generously. The Immigration Reform and Control Act of 1986 actually provided amnesty to some three million illegal immigrants, as long as they could show they had worked in this country for the last ninety days. And the Immigration Act of 1990 carried an economic agenda by encouraging the immigration of people with certain skills the country needs.

Now it's a different story. There's not enough work to go around. America needs her jobs for Americans. Does that mean we should stem the tide of legal immigrants? Absolutely not. But it does mean that we need to get tougher, much tougher, on illegal immigrants.

Illegal immigrants take away American jobs. For every one hundred of them in the work force, sixty-five Americans lose their jobs. Right now illegal immigration is running unchecked in this country. By some counts, as many as three million illegal immigrants enter the United States each year. Of these, about 250,000 to 300,000 stay on to look for work and/or welfare benefits. Unfortunately, they are all too successful at both. An ample supply of low- or no-skill jobs in the agricultural, garment, construction, retail, and automotive parts industries provides plenty of labor for illegal immigrants.

How do these people take away American jobs? When an employer hires an illegal immigrant to glue rhinestones onto garments for $4 an hour, cash, an American worker is left standing idle.

How else? When employers have access to a pool of laborers willing to do work at substandard wages, and in many instances dangerous or unhealthy conditions, they have no incentive to upgrade the work into a job with a living wage for Americans. And in this way, illegal immigrants stifle job creation.

The Reality

Not only do illegal immigrants stifle job creation, but in the process they institutionalize an underworld of sweatshop labor in this country. For example:

- In Chicago, Polish workers were hired to rip asbestos-laden insulation material from schools and other public buildings. Against federal rules that require four breaks, these workers labor for six and a half hours nonstop. Against federal rules that require three changes of clothing daily, these workers labor in the same outfit all day.

- At a flower farm in Ventura County, California, hundreds of Mexicans were held behind barbed wire to labor sixteen hours a day for subminimum wages and then made to buy food from the grower at inflated prices. In an ensuing federal indictment, it was found that workers who labored more than 160 hours sometimes *owed* money to their employer.

- In El Paso, Texas, Mexican workers showed up for work on payday to find the factory closed. Wages totaling $85,000 were owed, but never paid.

But when employer sanctions, or the threat of employer sanctions (created by the 1986 reform act), for hiring illegal immigrants are applied, working conditions improve and opportunities for Americans increase. For example:

- To avoid sanctions, one farmer in California's Central Valley made work more palatable for legal immigrants and Americans by planting six-foot peach trees that could be harvested without the use of a ladder.
- A California strawberry grower sought to retain workers by creating a work rotation and shortening the workday.
- A personnel agency owner reported in *Western Food Service* magazine that wages rose by as much as 30 percent after the 1986 Immigration Reform Act took hold.

What You Can Do

Avoid hiring illegal immigrants. The wages might be cheaper, but in the long run, it costs American jobs.

Report those who do. If you are aware of a company that is exploiting illegal immigrants, report it. To do this, call the United States Immigration and Naturalization Service. The telephone number is in the blue pages of almost every telephone book. All reports are anonymous. If the company is found to be hiring and employing illegal immigrants, fines can range from $250 to $10,000 for each worker.

Write to Washington. Immigration is a passionate topic among lawmakers both for and against stricter immigration laws. But they need to know how you feel. Write and tell them illegal immigrants are depleting American jobs and that you feel more funds should be provided for border patrol and enforcement activities. See Chapter 4 for how to deliver an effective and powerful letter.

How to Spend Your Money to Generate American Jobs

8

Think Globally, Buy Locally

Buying locally puts your dollars to work
saving American jobs.

OVERVIEW

Buying American can be a daunting assignment. There's always the chance that you will purchase an RCA television only to discover that the company's sets are made by a foreign corporation.

By buying locally, from businesses located within your town, city, state, or region, you pump important capital back into the community where you live, work, and play. Your purchases go directly to supporting the jobs and standards of living of the people who mean the most to you—family and friends.

Here are all the other good reasons to buy locally.

1. You can be reasonably confident that the manufacturers paid taxes, and that they presumably complied with state and federal environmental regulations. After all, U.S. manufacturers must comply with more environmental regulations than any country in the world.

2. When you buy the products grown, crafted, or manufactured in your own town, city, or state, you can be sure the company wasn't exploiting workers by using child or slave labor—an allegation leveled at China and many Third World manufacturers.

3. And buying locally can create ripples of prosperity that affect the economic seas of an entire region.

A Brief Case Study

Michael and Julie Holahan are pioneers of sorts in the buy-local phenomenon. In 1987, after trying to decide how to diversify their lunch-box catering business, which they operated from Philadelphia's Reading Terminal Market, one of the last remaining urban farmers' markets, the Holahans came up with a new idea.

"Christmas was approaching, and Julie and I decided to expand the business by marketing gift baskets," remembers Michael. "We needed something different and settled on a 'Pennsylvania Foods' theme."

Just about everyone warned them against trying their business to only one state's products. "We were told that consumers didn't care where products came from, they only want the best quality at the best price."

But the Holahans persevered. They scoured the state to find locally made apple butter, handmade train whistles, and Amish quilts and crafts. The quality surpassed anything they had imagined. So, too, did customer reaction.

"We discovered that there is a lot of interest in locally produced products," says Michael. "The problem is that most people—ourselves included at first—don't know which products come from their own backyards." Michael Holahan understands that his business isn't likely to make or break a supplier or manufacturer. But the business does create jobs, especially in the state's rural communities, which need them the most. And the impact has been exponential.

"One day the buyer of a large local department store came by our booth and started copying down the names of the products we carried," says Michael. "A few weeks later, the store launched a department similar to our store."

Since starting the business, the Holahans have shipped baskets throughout the world, to as far away as Anchorage, Paris, and Riyadh.

What You Can Do

- **Patronize retailers throughout the country that carry only local products.** The quality is often higher than similar imported products. "Made in Oregon," "The Louisiana

General Store," and "South Dakota Select" are but a few examples.

- **Call your local chamber of commerce and your state or city chamber of commerce.** They often publish lists of locally produced foods, products, and even services.

- **Contact your state Department of Agriculture.** It is likely to know of local orchards, honey producers, pick-your-own strawberry farms, and dairies where you can buy locally and enjoy a family outing at the same time.

- **Be on the lookout for special promotions that advertise local products.** KDKA-TV in Pittsburgh, KYW-TV in Philadelphia, WCAX-TV in Vermont, and KGW-TV in Oregon have sponsored advertising promotions that feature local businesses in an attempt to inform consumers of their products.

- **Attend local arts and crafts fairs and shows.** That's where you can find local artists and craftspeople to support through your purchases.

- **Help spur demand for local goods and services through your local church or civic association.** Ask members to contribute lists of locally produced products. Publish the list in your organization's newsletter. Contact the businesses and ask them to discount their products in exchange for local patronage.

- **Follow press coverage of local businesses.** The media often profiles local companies and their products. It might surprise you just how many products come from your own backyard.

Food for Thought

"We live in a world of contradictions. As much as we embrace the global economy, we still live in whatever smallest unit defines our life—family, neighborhood, and community," says Michael Holahan, founder of the Pennsylvania General Store. "It should be our priority to support our community and our neighbors first. Then as our own areas prosper, we can expand our reach out and purchase goods and services elsewhere in the country."

9

Saving Jobs by Shopping at Home

Catalog shopping is easy, convenient, and supports regional and American-made products that put Americans to work.

OVERVIEW

One of the obstacles to buying American is that most sales-clerks in department and other stores know little about the products they sell. Catalogs, on the other hand, give much more information to customers and often include the country of origin in the short blurbs that accompany each item. One other advantage: FTC regulations require catalog marketers to include the country of origin in advertising for textiles and other apparel.

Catalog marketers also typically provide employment to Americans in rural areas, where jobs are most needed. For instance, L.L. Bean is located in Freeport, Maine. Lands' End is in Dodgeville, Wisconsin. Southwest Indian Foundation's catalog comes from Gallup, New Mexico. All these companies are significant employers in their hometowns.

Facts and Figures

Catalog shopping has become an obsession for many Americans. And why not? We invented it. It was Mr. Sears, Mr. Roebuck, Mr. Montgomery, and Mr. Ward who first used this marketing method as a way to get products to isolated frontiersmen. Today:

- Catalog sales have become a $50 billion-a-year industry and are still growing, by just under 10 percent a year.
- Employment in the catalog industry surpassed 250,000 in 1990 and 1991, an increase of about 16 percent over 1987 levels.
- Total employment in the catalog industry grew from 950,000 in 1987 to 1.17 million Americans in 1991.

What You Can Do

Use catalogs to buy American. The big advantage of catalogs is that most are supported by toll-free 800 numbers that you can call for further information regarding advertised products. When we randomly called twenty catalog marketers, five of the service representatives told us immediately where a product we wanted to buy was produced. Five of the operators put us on hold for up to three minutes before getting back to us with the answer. The remaining operators gave us toll numbers to call to get the information.

Not a bad showing when you compare that response to the puzzled looks most store clerks give when asked about a product.

Use catalogs to buy difficult-to-find, regional products. Catalogs can also allow you to buy American-made products unavailable in your neck of the woods. The Vermont Country Store catalog, for instance, can deliver Vermont maple syrup right to your door.

Catalogs You Should Get to Know

L.L. Bean, the Maine-based catalog marketer of outdoor wear and products, wins the award for the most aggressively pro-American cataloger. Seventy-five percent of its products are made here in the United States. The company's 99.9 percent record of correctly filling orders has won it kudos and made it one of the most efficient and effective marketers in America. Its flagship store, based on Main Street in Freeport, Maine, serves as a monument to the great American outdoorsman and features an indoor trout pond and on-site demonstrations from American craftspeople.

Many catalogs feature their own product line, made in their USA factories, in addition to other items. They can tell you which products are their own line and which products were made by other manufacturers. Some of the catalogs that are heavy on American-made products include:

TOOLS

Bridge City Tool Works
1104 Northeast 28th Street
Portland, Oregon 97232
800-253-3332

Levenger Tools for Serious
Readers
975 South Congress Avenue
Delray Beach, Florida
33445-4628
800-544-0880

FURNITURE

Yield House (all furniture
made in Conway, New
Hampshire)

America's Country Home
P.O. Box 5000
North Conway, New
Hampshire 03860-5000
800-258-4720

REGIONAL PRODUCTS

The Vermont Country Store
Mail Order Office
P.O. Box 3000
Manchester Center, Vermont
05255-3000
802-362-2400

Southwest Indian Foundation
P.O. Box 86
Gallup, New Mexico
87302-0001
505-863-4037

CLOTHING

L.L. Bean, Inc.
Freeport, Maine 04033-0001
800-221-4221

Lands' End Direct Merchants
1 Lands' End Way
Dodgeville, Wisconsin 53595
800-356-4444

Huntington Clothiers
(most items made in
Columbus; a few
imported items)
1285 Alum Creek Drive
Columbus, Ohio 43209
800-848-6203

The Black Dog (informal
and funky clothing,
much of it made in
America) *
Martha's Vineyard
Beach Street Extension
P.O. Box 2219
Vineyard Haven,
Massachusetts 02568

THE ARTS AND PRESERVATION

National Wildlife Federation
Order/Contribution
Department
8925 Leesburg Pike
Vienna, Virginia 22184-0001
800-432-6564 (orders)

Winterthur
Museum and Garden
Catalogue Division
100 Enterprise Place
Dover, Delaware 19901
800-767-0500

GIFTS

Country Manor
Route 211, P.O. Box 520
Sperryville, Virginia 22740
800-344-8354

Sources

Consult the Catalog of Catalogs. It's available at the reference
desk of most libraries.

10

We Will Not Be Concorde

The next time someone says America can't compete,
tell them about U.S. beers and wines.
They are the best in the world.

OVERVIEW

You've heard the rap: America simply doesn't produce the quality products the world wants or expects. If that's so, how do you explain the success of the U.S. beer and wine industries in playing to the world's most discriminating palates? American brewers and vintners have done a remarkable job of producing world-class products. Trouble is, too many Americans don't realize it. They still grab a St. Pauli Girl or Beck's over Samuel Adams Boston Lager, even though many industry insiders claim that imports add refined sugar and processed corn to appeal to American tastes. Samuel Adams, on the other hand, has consistently won blind taste tests against all comers, imported and domestic.

As far as wines go, California vintners regularly rack up best-of awards in such publications as *The Wine Spectator*. Washington State, which is touted as the big up-and-coming area of U.S. wine production, is gaining praise for a number of its recent vintages.

So why don't our brewers and vintners rank high in the minds of American consumers? Too often Americans, especially those with a few dollars in their pockets, equate quality with imports. It's the old notion that if it comes from far away, it has to be better. Well, that kind of thinking has to stop, especially among American consumers who argue against buy-

American, and who insist that quality, not country of origin, should be the only determinant for buying a product.

Facts and Figures

- The U.S. beer industry generates about $170 billion in revenue each year and employs 904,800 Americans. When you add in secondary jobs in retailing and wholesaling generated by the brewing industry, employment jumps to 2.7 million Americans.
- The American wine industry contributes about $32 billion of economic activity to the American economy. It's responsible for employing about 530,000 Americans.
- U.S. exports of wine increased more than 19 percent from 1989 to 1990, mainly because of the quality of the product now being produced in this country.
- If in one day, two million Americans stopped buying imported beer and instead picked up a bottle of Brooklyn Beer—a highly touted domestic brew—it would create 5,000 American jobs in New York State.
- The Japanese are in love with Brooklyn Beer, brewed in Boston, Pittsburgh, and Oregon. It is air-shipped overnight to Tokyo bars and sells for as much as $13 a bottle!

The American Beers That Beat the World

How do American beers compare against imports? "Great," according to Jay Brandt of Brandt's Market and Cafe, St. Louis, cosponsor of the Brandt's/Riddle International Beer Tasting, now in its seventh year. The contest consists of two tastings, one a blind taste test conducted by a panel of twelve brew masters and beer experts, the second involving 250 consumers.

In the blind test, Samuel Adams won top honors in the light/lager category. Pete's Wicked Ale, a micro-brew from Palo Alto, California, took top honors in the ales/amber category.

Of the fifty beers in competition, fifteen American brews won first-place awards in each category of blind testing.

The consumer tests identified Crazy Horse Malt Liquor, from Baltimore, as the top beer.

The American Wines That Shine

In the Intervin Competition, a highly respected wine-tasting competition that pits American and Canadian wines against foreign producers, domestic vintages not only held their own, they actually captured more gold medals than any other country—thirty-three in all, compared to twenty-two by the Australians, nine by the Canadians, and only one by the French.

Two gold medal winning wines at the 1991 American Wine Society were 1987 Blanc De Noirs Napa Valley from the S. Anderson Vineyard in California and 1984 Collectors Series Cabernet Sauvignon from Ste. Chappelle Winery in Idaho.

In the most recent rankings of the one hundred best wines, published by *The Wine Spectator*, 1987 Caymus Cabernet Sauvignon Napa Valley Special Selection was named the third-best wine in the world and 1987 Chateau Montelena Napa Valley Cabernet Sauvignon placed eighth.

New Trends

Microbreweries are hot. These small breweries, which are usually connected to a pub, are popping up throughout the country—an estimated 274 now dot the American landscape. The popularity is understandable: they produce some of the best beer in the world. Want to find one near you? Call the Association of Brewers at 303-447-0816.

What You Can Do

Support American brewers and vintners by buying their products. There's no excuse not to: their quality is impressive.

Make an American beer or wine your signature drink. Instead of serving Heineken or French wines, choose Samuel Adams and a Washington State vintage. You would be surprised how many people you can influence to do likewise simply by serving the best America has to offer.

Visit local wineries and sample their wares. Pennsylvania, Ohio, Massachusetts, New York, Idaho, Washington State, Virginia, and other states all have thriving wineries where you can spend a day enjoying the scenery and buy 100 percent American products.

Gold Medal Winners of the 1992 Great American Beer Festival

Classic Pale Ale
Sierra Nevada Pale Ale, Sierra Nevada Brewing Co., Chico, California.

India Pale Ale
Solstice Ale, Hubcap Brewery & Kitchen, Vail, Colorado.

American Pale/Amber Ale
McTarnahan's Ale, Portland Brewing Co., Portland, Oregon.

Traditional Bitter
Moon Dog Ale, Great Lakes Brewing Co., Cleveland, Ohio.

Scottish Ales
Sonoma Irish Ale, Sonoma Brewing Co., Petaluma, California.

Blonde Ale
Prime Time, Big Time Brewing Co., Seattle, Washington.

Porter
Boulder Porter, Boulder Beer, Boulder, Colorado.

Dry Stout
Stout, Butterfield Brewing Co., Fresno, California.

Sweet Stout
Seabright Oatmeal Stout, Seabright Brewery, Santa Cruz, California.

Barley Wine
Sierra Nevada Bigfoot Barleywine Ale, Sierra Nevada Brewing Co., Chico, California.

Fruit, Vegetable
Passion Pale, Tied House Cafe, Alameda, California.

Herb, Spice
Celis White, Celis Brewery, Austin, Texas.

Specialty
Trippel Threat, Cambridge Brewing Co., Cambridge, Massachusetts.

Smoke-Flavored
Alaskan Smoked Porter, Alaskan Brewing & Bottling Co., Douglas, Alaska.

Bock
Frankenmuth German Style Bock, Frankenmuth Brewery, Frankenmuth, Michigan.

Dark Lager
Schwarz Hacker, Rock Bottom Brewery, Denver, Colorado.

Munchner Helles & Dortmunder Export
Export Gold, Stoudt Brewing Co., Adamstown, Pennsylvania.

European Pilsner
Legacy Lager, Chicago Brewing Co., Chicago, Illinois.

American Lager
Schlitz, The Stroh Brewery Co., Detroit, Michigan.

American Light Lager
Michelob Light, Anheuser-Busch, St. Louis, Missouri.

American Premium Lager
Lowenbrau Regular, Miller Brewing Co., Milwaukee, Wisconsin.

American Dry Lager
Keystone Dry, Coors Brewing Co., Golden, Colorado.

American Malt Liquor
Olde English 800 Malt Liquor, Pabst Brewing, Milwaukee, Wisconsin.

Dusseldorf Altbier
Samuel Adams Boston Stock Ale, Boston Beer Co., Boston, Massachusetts.

American Lager/Ale Cream Ale
Scrimshaw Beer, North Coast Brewing Co., Fort Bragg, California.

German Wheat
Hopsi Hafe-Weizen, Hopsi Bistro & Brewery, Scottsdale, Arizona.

American Wheat
Marin Hefe Weiss, Marin Brewing Co., Larkspur, California.
Marzen/Oktoberfest
Fest, Stoudt Brewing Co., Adamstown, Pennsylvania.
Vienna
Brooklyn Lager, The Brooklyn Brewing Co., Brooklyn, New
York.
English Brown Ale
PMD Mild Ale, Goose Island Brewing Co., Chicago, Illinois.
American Brown Ale
Pete's Wicked Ale, Pete's Brewing Co., Palo Alto, California.

Beware of Imposters

In her book *Buy American: A How-To-Handbook*, author An-
nette L. Donoho identifies these seemingly American spirits
that are actually owned by foreign companies:

Beers	*Wines*
Black Label	Almaden Vineyards
Colt 45	Christian Brothers
Iron City	Inglenook
Lone Star	Monterey Vineyards
Rainier	Napa Ridge
Rolling Rock	
Schmidt's	

11

Over Here, Not Over There

Want to spur job creation?
Take an American vacation.

OVERVIEW

Americans love to travel. Maybe it's our appreciation of freedom, or our fondness for the open road. Whatever accounts for it, the American love affair with travel, tourism, and vacationing has spawned this nation's second-largest employer of people, right after health care. Surprised? A lot of Americans are, especially those who crave a Caribbean honeymoon or a ski trip to the Alps. After all, the best vacations take you to exotic places in faraway lands. Or are they? Consider this. Non-Americans flock in greater numbers to the United States to vacation than they do to any other country. New York City, Los Angeles, Washington, D.C., San Francisco, Miami, Orlando, Las Vegas, and other top U.S. vacation spots are classified as mega-destinations by the international travel industry, attracting more than forty million foreigners each year.

Overseas, a trip to the States is viewed as the ultimate in cachet. And foreigners don't just come here to see the big draws. They also land here to enjoy roadside America, those quirky, small, out-of-the-way places that make this country unique. In fact, in Germany, one of the most prized vacations is a bus tour through the heartland of the United States of America. Their German guides/bus drivers, who have conducted similar tours throughout the world, call America the most accessible and beautiful touring country in the world.

But given a chance, many Americans still opt to vacation outside of the country, resulting in a yearly loss of about $40 billion. Some of this loss is unavoidable, such as businesspeople seeing overseas clients. But most of the straying of Americans to other lands results from the misguided belief that the best vacations are over there, not over here.

The Importance of Travel to Our Economy

- In 1990, spending on travel services in the United States reached approximately $327.3 billion.

- The travel and tourism industry is the third-largest retail industry in the country, after automotive dealers and food stores.

- Americans spend more on travel than on clothing, accessories, jewelry, and personal care combined, and more than on household utilities, including telephone services.

- Tourism makes up about 6 percent of the GNP and 17 percent of the service sector.

- Some 5.85 million Americans were employed in the travel industry in 1990.

- Since 1972, payroll jobs in travel-related businesses have more than doubled, while total U.S. payroll employment has increased by less than 50 percent.

- Each $53,300 spent by travelers directly supports one new job.

What You Can Do

Make America your destination. The evidence is overwhelming: America offers the best tourist attractions in the world. But sadly, more Americans have visited countries overseas than have visited their own capital.

Thinking of taking that dream vacation? Here are some of the U.S. destinations that can compete with any on earth:

★ Taos, New Mexico. If you think the French or Italian Alps offer the world's best skiing, think again. With seventy-one slopes and powered-whipped by Rocky Mountain winds, those in the know are now touting Taos as the place to be if you love to ski.

Dadou Mayer knows firsthand. A former competitive skier for France, Mayer relocated to Taos in 1958. He has since opened his own bed and breakfast, Salsa Del Salto, to cater to skiers from around the globe.

"We have our regular domestic and European or South American customers," says Mayer. "Sometimes they say they are going to try foreign resorts. I tell them to go ahead because they will be back."

Mayer says that Taos offer the charm, beauty, and challenge of European ski resorts without the throngs of people, long lines, and outrageous prices. For instance, a room at his bed and breakfast costs only $100 a night, compared to $250 at similar accommodations in the Alps.

For more information, write:

New Mexico Tourism Department
Joseph M. Montoya Building
1100 St. Francis Drive
Santa Fe, New Mexico 87503

Or

Taos County Chamber of Commerce
229 Paseo Del Pueblo Sur, Drawer I
Taos, New Mexico 87571
505-758-3873

You can make reservations at Dadou Mayer's Salsa Del Salto by calling 505-776-2422

★ Hot Springs, Arkansas. Sure it's the boyhood home of President Bill Clinton, but it's also the spa capital of the country—competing against such legendary hot springs as France's Le Boulou and Salins-Les Bains.

Hot Springs National Park and the bathhouses surrounding it use the geo-heated waters of a 4,000-year-old underground spring to rejuvenate, relax, and pamper more than two million visitors each year. The forty-seven hot springs are among the purest in the world, with water temperatures ranging from 100 to 105 degrees.

Best of all, because the springs are located in a national park, the prices are regulated, so the average treatment is about $20. A typical visit includes a ninety-minute bath, a loofah massage given by a personal attendant, a drink of the springs' mythical waters, plus various showers, body wraps, and hot and cold compress applications.

One last note: the Japanese, with their tradition of communal baths, love this place and are among its most loyal patrons.

To learn more, write:

Hot Springs Convention and Visitors Bureau
134 Convention Boulevard
Hot Springs, Arkansas 71902
800-772-2489

★ New Orleans French Quarter. A jet-set vacation for many Americans is Rio de Janeiro during Mardi Gras. In fact, Brazil was the sixth most popular tourist destination for Americans in 1990. But in case you haven't heard, Rio is racked with crime. Armed gangs walk the streets and room occupancy has fallen to 50 percent.

The alternative? New Orleans. Sure, it's naughty and sometimes gaudy. But the city sure does know how to throw a party, especially during Mardi Gras, which runs from Christmas to the beginning of the Lenten season, with the most celebrated parties and parades taking place the week before Ash Wednesday. The city receives more than eight million tourists a year. And according to Maureen Detweiler, a spokesperson for New Orleans Mardi Gras, Rio's fall has been New Orleans's gain, with more and more Americans choosing to celebrate closer to home and away from Brazilian crime.

For Mardi Gras information, write:

> Greater New Orleans Tourist and Convention Commission
> 1520 Sugar Bowl Drive
> New Orleans, Louisiana 70112
> 504-566-5011

★ San Diego, California. A national jewel of tourism, San Diego offers a rich mix of beaches and attractions that can't be beat—anywhere. Its zoo is world-renowned, a daylong adventure guaranteed to enthrall even the most difficult youngsters.

The region's seventy miles of Pacific beaches are often compared to the French Riviera, with one major difference—they are cleaner and better maintained. Costs are exceedingly reasonable. Room rates start at $45 and climb to $345. The city's dry, comfortable climate nurtures an incredible array of palms, flowers, and greenery. Two sparkling bays, several uplifting mountains, a nearby desert, and an international border combine to make San Diego one of this country's best vacation destinations.

For more information, write:

> San Diego Convention and Visitors Bureau
> Department 700
> 200 Third Avenue, Suite 824
> San Diego, California 92101-4190
> 619-236-1212

★ Vermont. Sure the skiing is great. But the summer attractions are nearly as appealing. Vermont bicycling has been rated better than that found in the Alps. The countryside, which strongly resembles that of Germany, offers one of the least-developed areas left in the Northeastern United States.

"Europeans are amazed at how pristine the state is," says Bud McLaughlin, owner of the Mountain Top Inn and Resort in Chittenden. Ten percent of the resort's business is made up of European vacationers. "Foreigners can't believe that you can look off a mountaintop and not see a single building. It's not like that in Europe."

For more information, write:

Mountain Top Inn and Resort
Mountain Top Road
Chittendon, Vermont 05737
802-483-2311

Or

Vermont Travel Division
802-828-3236

★ Hawaii. It's now the tourist destination of choice for Japanese travelers, who are willing to forgo closer tropical paradises to experience what more Americans need to know: Hawaii offers that perfect combination of tropical wonder with world-class comfort and accommodations.

While the big island is full of hustle and bustle, the island of Kauai has been rated better than Tahiti for its number of safe and uncrowded beaches. The state's well-tended highways make it easy to explore by car or bus.

For more information, write:

Hawaii Visitors Bureau
Waikiki Business Plaza
2270 Kalakaua Avenue, 8th Floor
Honolulu, Hawaii 96815
808-923-1811

The Top Ten

Here's where foreigners go when they visit America:

1. New York City
2. Los Angeles
3. San Francisco
4. Miami
5. Orlando
6. Washington, D.C.
7. Las Vegas
8. Boston
9. Chicago
10. San Diego

12

Franchise Wise

You can support American jobs by buying franchised products and services.

OVERVIEW

One of the hottest U.S. exports isn't a product at all—it's a way of doing business. Franchising and American franchised businesses are hotly pursued by foreign investors impressed by American know-how for running everything from frozen yogurt stores to video rental outlets.

Why all the interest? American franchisers are some of the best service businesses in the world. They deliver a quality and consistency of product that's hard to beat—anywhere, by anyone.

And rightly so. After all, franchising was invented in this country, by guys like Howard Johnson. But it wasn't until Ray Kroc stumbled upon a San Bernardino drive-in restaurant operated by the McDonald brothers that the marketing system caught fire and transformed the American economy.

Today, franchising is routinely cited as a pillar of the American economy, accounting for more than one-third of all retail sales. Best of all, most franchise companies are American-owned, American-operated, and employ millions of American workers.

Facts and Figures

According to a recent survey by the International Franchise Association:

48

- Franchising is now a part of more than sixty industries and employs seven million people.
- Gross receipts from franchised businesses topped $340 billion in 1991.
- American franchise companies are expanding overseas at an astounding rate, a phenomenon that pumps capital back into this country via franchise fees and royalty payments. More than one-third of recently surveyed U.S. franchise companies support overseas units. Ninety-three percent of these companies plan to increase their presence overseas.

Fast food and automotive services are only two heavily franchised industries. Just about every kind of business imaginable is now franchised in one form or another, including residential and commercial cleaning firms, print shops, office supply retailers, convenience stores, magazines and newspapers, even law firms and dental clinics.

BUSINESS OPPORTUNITIES IN FRANCHISING

Franchising plays another important role in American job creation: it puts entrepreneurs in business, who in turn hire other Americans.

If you're thinking of starting a business, franchising is well worth considering. If you are interested in a particular business and want to know if it's a franchise, just ask the manager or owner. He or she can usually answer you immediately and tell you whether the home office is based in this country.

Franchising is one of the safest ways to start a business. According to the International Franchise Association, while approximately 60 percent of all new businesses shut their doors during the first five years of operation, only about 3 percent of franchised businesses suffer the same fate.

What accounts for this success? Franchising is a cloning game. A franchise company takes an existing, successful business and then replicates it by teaching investors (franchisees) everything they need to know to operate the business. Because franchise companies live off their franchisees by taking a small percentage of their sales, they have an ongoing incentive to spur them to succeed.

This formula accounts for why McDonald's is now the world's largest chain of restaurants, with more than 12,250 locations worldwide.

Sources

If you're thinking of getting into franchising, the International Franchise Association publishes a full library of books and pamphlets on the topic. Call the organization at 202-628-8000 for a listing of its publications.

13

The TV Tragedy

The only remaining U.S. television manufacturer is hanging by a thread. Should we help Zenith? Yes.

OVERVIEW

No story of an American fall from dominance is more disturbing than the destruction of the U.S. television industry. The United States, once the world leader in TV design, research, and production, has seen over the past two decades virtually every one of its television makers either sold to foreign competitors or driven out of business. The names read like an American Hall of Fame: Philco, Emerson, Magnavox, Sylvania, Westinghouse, Motorola—all have now gone out of business or overseas. The only remaining U.S. television company, Zenith, has struggled valiantly, but even it has moved much of its production to Mexico. While Zenith still employs 6,000 Americans near Chicago, the company is teetering on bankruptcy, and at this writing is warning that it will have serious cash flow problems if it can't renegotiate its bank credit.

How We Lost the TV Industry

Pat Choate, author of *Agents of Influence*, argues that the industry's downfall was due to "sustained, predatory attacks by a cartel of Japanese television manufacturers operating with the knowledge and support of the Japanese government."

In compelling detail, Choate has reported on how the cartel closed Japan's markets to American-made TVs and then, using profits from its sales in Japan, financed the dumping of its TVs here in America. The cartel even went so far as to establish secret payments to American importers that allowed its TVs to be sold at below production costs.

The result, argues Zenith, is that the domestic television industry was devastated by severe price erosion for its products. Zenith, for instance, has not reported a full-year profit since 1984. It moved production to Mexico as a last-ditch effort to reduce labor costs and stay in business.

That's unfortunate, because Zenith produces good-quality televisions. *Consumer Reports*, not exactly a booster of American jobs or American companies, ranked Zenith's SJ2071W 20-inch set the clearest picture in its class, and Zenith's 13-inch SJ1325W also rated well.

What You Can Do

Buy Zenith. Zenith has moved much of its manufacturing facilities to overseas locations, but the company is still recognized as the only American television manufacturer in the market today. In that regard, dollars generated by the sale of Zenith products do flow back to the company's headquarters near Chicago. So we should support the company and its products. After all, America deserves at least one company in a field it pioneered and excelled in.

Support Philips Consumer Electronics. Philips Consumer Electronics, a division of a Dutch company, produces television sets here in Tennessee. According to company spokesperson John Castle, about 80 percent of the dollar value of each domestically produced set comes from American-made components, which he believes is the highest percentage of any television manufacturer. Philips has also agreed to produce high-definition TVs (HDTV) in this country, if its format is the one chosen for the new technology.

14

Putting One American to Work for 1.7 Years

Want to generate American jobs?
Start with the housing industry.

OVERVIEW

The housing industry is a prime generator of jobs in this country. Six to seven million Americans work directly in the housing industry. When you add in indirect employment associated with the housing industry—or people working to make windows, insulation, and doors—you have an industry that employs ten to twelve million Americans.

No wonder housing is the best barometer of our economic well-being. When times are good, the housing industry employs millions of people in trades, architecture, sales, and the banking industry. When times are bad, everyone suffers.

There are many Americans who can afford homes but don't own them. The reasons are many. Some don't think they earn enough to qualify for a mortgage. Others are comfortable living in an apartment or condominium and see no reason to move.

But buying a home is one of the single most effective ways you can create jobs for your fellow Americans. The average-size new home puts one American to work for 1.7 years! And home ownership is a great investment. The annualized total return on home purchases has been about 7 percent since 1960. During the past three decades, the major source of personal wealth for many Americans has been the appreciation in the value of their homes. Need some additional convincing? Then consider some quick statistics.

Facts and Figures

- Construction of new homes accounts for 4 to 5 percent of our gross national product. Add in the cost of repairs and renovations to existing homes and the industry generates 13 to 15 percent of our nation's total economic output.
- A large development of 1,000 new homes generates 1,759 worker years of employment, $45.7 million in wages, and $18.8 million in tax revenue.
- According to the National Association of Realtors and the United States Census Bureau, each house that is sold contributes between $15,000 and $20,000 to the gross domestic product (GDP).

Where to Begin

Your local banker can give you an idea of how much home you can afford and lay out some strategies for buying one. Realtors are another good source. According to Forrest Pafenberg, director of real estate finance at the National Association of Realtors, today's real estate sales professionals know more than ever about financing options. They can often provide an objective opinion on whether you can afford to buy a home.

According to Pafenberg, the key to home ownership is first getting into the market. "It's much easier to buy a bigger or newer home once you have bought a first home. That's why it's imperative for young people or prospective first-time home buyers to start saving now for a down payment that could get them into a home of their own."

Special Tips

By forgoing the purchase of a new car and instead saving $175 a month for five years, you would have enough for a down payment on a $100,000 home.

Also, when good fortune strikes, put the money toward buying a home. Tax refunds, inheritances, and company bonuses are excellent sources for financing the down payment on a new home.

Books on Buying a New Home

Buy Your First Home Now. Peter Miller. Harper & Row Publishers, Inc., New York.

J. K. *Lasser's Guide to Buying Your First Home.* Joseph Catalino. Prentice Hall, New York.

15

Put America on Your Shopping List

Is the loss of American jobs tough to swallow? You can do your bit, three times a day and between meals.

OVERVIEW

For most Americans, a trip to the grocery store is a weekly ritual. And every time you go, you could help to create American jobs. But does it matter when you buy grocery store items made in America by American companies?

It does for people like Linda Menicheschi. Linda works for Hershey Foods Corporation in Hershey, Pennsylvania, the small town where Hershey chocolate bars are made and where the lamp posts are shaped like Hershey Kisses. Linda started out twenty-three years ago, as a clerk in the plant training department. Since then, she has been promoted and now she is a contract manager, evaluating manufacturing opportunities for her employer.

In many ways, her career with Hershey has been the anchor for her life. "At one point, I was a single parent" says Linda. "My job provided a lot of security. Hershey has done extremely well, and treats its employees fairly. I was never concerned about not having a job. Sure, we might have had to downsize at some point, but I knew that the process would be well managed and accomplished through attrition." However, it was more than just security. Hershey sent Linda to college, gave her the ability to send her son Jason to Hofstra University, and gave her the ability to purchase a primary and a vacation home.

56

"My job at Hershey's has meant a lot to me" says Linda. "In general, I think that the productivity and the work ethic is good, and there is something to be said for keeping the jobs here in America. I think there are many social things that we pay for through the workplace, but that we all benefit from them."

What You Can Do

Put America on your shopping list. You have to be aware of who makes what. For the record, here's some consumer products and companies that seem American but are really foreign-owned.

Grand Metropolitan, PLC, a British company, owns these companies or sells these products:

Green Giant	Alpo
Pillsbury	Burger King

Unilever, another British company, makes or promotes these brands:

Mrs. Butterworth's	Lipton
Popsicle	Wishbone
Good Humor	Dove
Q-Tips	Wisk
Aim, Pepsodent	Lifebuoy
Vaseline	

And Swiss giant Nestle SA has:

Quik	Toll House
Taster's Choice	Friskies
Lean Cuisine	Mighty Dog
Libby's	Stouffer's

The list goes on and on. France's BSN sells Dannon Yogurt, Thai-based Unicord sell Bumble Bee brand seafood, and the English company Cadbury Schweppes sells Sunkist-brand beverages.

With food it's not always a simple case of buying from

American-owned companies. Why? Many foreign-owned companies keep their manufacturing here in the United States. But what you do accomplish by buying from American companies is keeping the profits from your purchases here. And in this respect, Colgate toothpaste edges out Pepsodent and a Hershey chocolate bar is sweeter than a Cadbury.

How to Get Smarter

Read the labels. In general, according to the U.S. Customs Service, items that are manufactured outside of the United States must be clearly marked. However, there are many exceptions. For example, products made with materials manufactured outside of the United States, but that undergo "substantial transformation" when they get here are not required to disclose the origin of essential ingredients.

Ask your grocer. You might not suspect it, but often grocery store managers are walking encyclopedias on food. They can tell you a lot about the country of origin, ingredients, and the manufacturer. Ask a question and you might find yourself in the middle of a dissertation.

Call the telephone numbers on the product labels. Fortunately, most food products manufactured by large corporations carry a toll-free number for questions or comments (see Chapter 6). Call the number and learn more about the products that you buy.

A Final Thought

Don't hesitate to buy fruit out of season, just because it comes from another country. That keeps our agricultural trade with other nations healthy. But, to help safeguard American jobs, buy more fruit when it's in season and grown locally or regionally. If you're not sure, ask your grocery store manager.

16

Collecting American Jobs

Trains, planes, and automobiles—toys—and many other collectibles support an entire strata of American jobs.

OVERVIEW

It's one of those cruel ironies that just as American-made products are losing favor worldwide, American collectibles are gaining ground. Take, for instance, American-made toy pedal cars and fire engines of the forties and fifties. Once routinely thrown out, they are now going for thousands of dollars. And what's the hottest new collectible? The original hand illustrations, framed and matted, from classic American cartoons such as Bugs Bunny or Woody Woodpecker.

American art, folk art, and collectibles are big business in this country, providing full- and part-time employment for everyone from flea market enthusiasts to art gallery auctioneers. Collecting them is also an excellent way to make a statement about American-made products. After all, some older products are worth tons of money, and who knows which mundane purchases we make today could be valuable in years to come?

A Collection of Facts

Collecting is an informal industry, so figures are sometimes hard to find. But in 1976, the American Stamp Dealers Association estimated that the total revenues from collecting was some $300 million. And that was seventeen years ago! In 1988, the same association gathered facts about stamp dealers and found that on average, each dealer employs 2.4 persons.

And this is just for stamps. Trains are big. So are dolls, cards, comic books, coins, figurines, and toys.

"We know there are thousands of items to collect," says Dale Graham, publisher of *Antiques and Collecting Hobbies.* "Some hold nothing but sentimental value. Others are worth thousands of dollars to our economy."

Take trains. "There are some twenty-five to thirty thousand train collectors in the United States, and the Lionel train is the kingpin of the market," explains Harry Overtoom, director of the Collector's Club of America for Lionel Trains. "My hobby started when my son was three," he says. "Now I have six hundred engines and three thousand cars on display in my home. And each one has a story or a piece of American history behind it."

What You Can Do

Start collecting. It's a great way to make your own statement about the importance of things made American. And it also generates jobs in this country.

1. Collect something of genuine interest to you. Here are some American-made products you might want to consider (some of which are already valuable and some of which might become valuable): early personal computers; Zippo lighters; Amish-made quilts; Sears catalogs; Shaker furniture; Beta videotapes; *Wizard of Oz* memorabilia; PlaySkool toys; Texas Instrument calculators; handmade fishing lures; obscure magazines (and some that might soon become obscure, such as *Spy, Sassy, Self,* etc.); and Gulf War surplus.

2. Once you get into collecting, set a schedule for making new acquisitions. That way, you'll be sure to build your collections. "Probably the most satisfying aspect," says Graham, "is seeking out new pieces." And he adds, "Collectibles don't have to be worth thousands. Most aren't, but that doesn't mean they will never deliver a profit. Many objects do, but the serious collector should not count on this."

3. Make it a family collection. Collectibles offer parents and children the opportunity to learn about their country's history, including how its collectibles are made and what traditions are involved in their production.

More Information

Collector Information
  Bureau
2420 Burton SE
Grand Rapids, Michigan
  49456
616-942-9CIB

Collector's Club of
  America
(Lionel Trains)
P.O. 479
La Salle, Illinois 61301
606-268-1942

American Stamp
  Dealers Association
3 School Street, Suite
  205
Glen Cove, New York
  11542
516-759-7000

*Antiques and Collecting
  Hobbies*
1006 South Michigan
  Avenue
Chicago, Illinois 60605
312-939-4767

17

We Are What We Wear

*Some people think the textile industry only offers
sweatshop jobs that Americans don't really want anyway.
Think again.*

OVERVIEW

More than 500,000 jobs in the apparel and textile industry
have been lost to foreign manufacturers since 1979. The ripple
effect of this loss is almost incalculable. The prevailing myth is
that these are jobs for unskilled workers offering the kind of
wages only seen in Third World countries.But the reality is that
Third World conditions prevail in many regions here:

- The South Bronx in New York, Liberty City in Miami, and
West L.A. in Los Angeles have lots of people who need
and want to work.
- Fully 54 percent of America's work force over the age of 16
have only a high school degree *or less*.
- Many Americans would jump at the chance to earn the
wages and enjoy the benefits that textile industry jobs
offer.

According to the Crafted with Pride in the U.S.A. Council,
Inc., U.S consumers spend on average $849 a year for clothing.
Of this, some 60 percent is imported. Textile industry analysts
say that if every one of us seized back $30 from imports, 100,000
American textile and apparel jobs would be saved. Looking
forward: If every American consumer would buy just one $6
pair of American-made socks, we would save the jobs of 20,000
textile workers. If every American consumer bought a $30

American-made sweater, the savings could be 100,000 jobs. And if every American bought two pairs of $50 jeans and $50 worth of American-made shirts, we'd preserve or create jobs for 500,000 textile and apparel workers. We can take back every job that was lost. The power is in our hands, and the solution is so simple. Who are we taking these back for? Hardworking Americans like the one described below.

A Brief Case Study

American textile manufacturer Fruit of the Loom operates a total of fifty-three plants. Of these, forty-five are located inside the United States. The company's Jamestown, Kentucky plant employs 3,200 workers. One of them, Betty Fisher, forty-seven, has been there since she was nineteen years old.

For her first twenty years, Betty was a machine operator. Since then, she has been in quality control, spot-checking briefs. The plant where Betty works is one of the company's most productive, turning out some 225,000 garments weekly.

When you buy American products, it means something to people like Betty. "American clothing," she says, "helped me send my daughter to college, buy my home, and support my standard of living.

"Fruit of the Loom is the best thing that ever happened to this whole county," says Betty. "When I graduated from high school, Fruit of the Loom was the factory everybody talked about, where you could make good money. I couldn't afford to go to college; in those days most people were lucky to even go to high school. But it's gotten better every year. I have a pension plan, I get four weeks' paid vacation, paid holidays. I could not ask for any better. I plan to keep working as long as my health holds out." And as long as Americans keep buying American-made clothing.

What You Can Do

Read the label. By law, every piece of clothing sold in America comes with a tag that identifies the country of origin. By reading the label, you'll learn that there is quality American-made clothing available. You just have to look for it.

Complain. When you go shopping for clothes, and you are presented with a poor selection of American-made goods, complain to the store owner and manager. Tell them that it is difficult for you to patronize the store when most clothes it sells are made in other countries. Retailers are sensitive to customer comments and are anxious to accommodate consumers. If three customers complained every day to the same store manager, you better believe his or her buying habits would change.

Praise. When you see evidence of retailers' commitment to stocking American-manufactured goods, let them know you're pleased with their efforts. Retailers need to have their strategies and merchandising ideas validated.

Be on the lookout. Many clothes will say "Made in China" or "Made in R.O.C." When you see this, send up a red flag, and move along. Why? Read chapter 27 which discusses some aspects of China's prison labor system.

For the Committed

Sponsor a "Bag That Tag" competition through a civic organization such as a chamber of commerce, school, church, or youth group. Offer children prizes for bringing in the most "Made in the USA" labels. It's a great way to raise public awareness in your town on the need to buy American textiles.

And remember, if you organize such a competition, don't forget to call the local newspaper and let it know about the event. Chances are you will land an article, or at least a mention, for your efforts.

18

Cutting Through the New-Car Smoke Screen

Simple ways to determine if a car is American-made.

OVERVIEW

There's a lot of confusion about how difficult it is to determine whether a car is American-made or an import. Some people would want you to believe that it's so difficult to tell an American car from a foreign one that it's not even worth trying.

Who benefits from claims that it's too difficult to determine if a car is American? Foreign car manufacturers. They're the ones fanning the smoke screen. They don't want to lose your business.

But when you do your homework, you realize that it's very easy to determine whether a car is American-made or not. The Environmental Protection Agency publishes an annual list that identifies American-made vehicles.

The EPA uses a criterion that's so simple and sensible, it's difficult to believe that our own government developed it. The EPA doesn't look at individual cars. Instead, it considers the entire car line. If 75 percent or more of the value of the car line is attributable to American parts and labor, then the car is "American-made."

This eliminates Toyota and Honda—companies that have nominal production here and use that presence to claim that their cars are American-made. These cars might be assembled in the United States, but their parts come from Japan. When you consider these car lines as a whole, they in no way qualify as American-made products. But foreign manufacturers don't want you to know that. Instead, they would rather muddy the waters and discourage you from trying to find out what cars are made right here in the USA.

What You Can Do

Write to the Environmental Protection Agency for its list of American-made cars. The address is:

U.S. EPA
2565 Plymouth Road
Ann Arbor, Michigan 48105

Ask any car dealer for the EPA determination. Car dealers know whether the cars they sell meet EPA standards for domestic content. Don't let them double-talk you with examples of foreign cars that are assembled here.

Set your friends straight. Many Americans will argue that it's impossible to tell an American car from an import because auto parts come from all over and some foreign manufacturers have plants here. Set them straight by telling them what the U.S. government says is an American car.

News You Can Use

In case you don't want to send away for the EPA ratings, here's what you're likely to find. It's not too surprising. Cars with foreign nameplates are tagged imports; most General Motors, Ford, and Chrysler products are identified as domestic.

1991 AMERICAN-MADE CARS

Chrysler

ACCLAIM	SHADOW
DAYTONA	SHADOW CONVERTIBLE
DYNASTY	SPIRIT
LEBARON	SUNDANCE
LEBARON CONVERTIBLE	B150/B250 VAN 2WD
NEW YORKER	B150/B250 WAGON 2WD
NEW YORKER FIFTH AVE./	B350 VAN 2WD
IMPERIAL	B350 WAGON 2WD

CARAVAN 2WD	D100/D150 PICKUP 2WD
CARAVAN 4WD	D250 PICKUP 2WD
CHEROKEE 2WD	GRAND WAGONEER 4WD
CHEROKEE 4WD	TOWN & COUNTRY 2WD
COMANCHE PICKUP 2WD	VOYAGER 2WD
COMANCHE PICKUP 4WD	VOYAGER 4WD
DAKOTA CAB CHASSIS 2WD	WRANGLER 4WD
DAKOTA PICKUP 2WD	W100/W150 PICKUP 4WD
DAKOTA PICKUP 4WD	W250 PICKUP 4WD

Ford

CONTINENTAL	TEMPO
COUGAR	THUNDERBIRD
ESCORT	TOPAZ
ESCORT FS	TOWN CAR
ESCORT WAGON	TRACER
GRAND MARQUIS	TRACER WAGON
GRAND MARQUIS WAGON	AEROSTAR VAN ALL-WHEEL
LTD CROWN VICTORIA	DRIVE
LTD CROWN VICTORIA WAGON	AEROSTAR WAGON ALL-WHEEL
MARK VII	DRIVE
MUSTANG	RONCO 4WD
PROBE	EXPLORER 4WD
SABLE	F150 PICKUP 4WD
SABLE WAGON V6 A/C	F250 PICKUP 4WD
TAURUS	NAVAJO
TAURUS WAGON	RANGER PICKUP 4WD
TAURUS WAGON V6 A/C	

General Motors

BERETTA	CENTURY WAGON
BONNEVILLE	COMMERCIAL CHASSIS
BROUGHAM	CORSICA
CAMARO	CORVETTE
CAPRICE	CUSTOM CRUISER
CAPRICE WAGON	CUTLASS CALAIS
CAVALIER	CUTLASS CIERA
CAVALIER CONVERTIBLE	CUTLASS CRUISER
CAVALIER WAGON	CUTLASS SUPREME
CENTURY	EIGHTY-EIGHT

ELDORADO
FIREBIRD/TRANS AM
FLEETWOOD/DEVILLE
GRAND AM
GRAND PRIX
LESABRE
LUMINA
METRO
METRO LSI
METRO XFI
NINETY-EIGHT/TOURING
PARK AVENUE
PRIZM
REGATTA
REGAL
RIVIERA
ROADMASTER WAGON
SC
SEVILLE
SKYLARK
SL
SUNBIRD
SUNBIRD CONVERTIBLE
TROFEO/TORONADO
6000
6000 WAGON
APV 2WD
ASTRO AWD (CARGO)
ASTRO AWD (PASSENGER)
ASTRO 2WD (CARGO)
ASTRO 2WD (PASSENGER)
BRAVADA AWD
C1500 PICKUP 2WD
C1500 SIERRA 2WD
C2500 PICKUP 2WD

C2500 SIERRA 2WD
G10/20 SPORTVAN 2WD
G10/20 VAN 2WD
G15/25RALLY 2WD
G15/25 VANDURA 2WD
G30 SPORTVAN 2WD
G30 VAN 2WD
G35 RALLY 2WD
G35 VANDURA 2WD
JIMMY SONOMA 2WD
JIMMY SONOMA 4WD
K1500 PICKUP 4WD
K1500 SIERRA 4WD
K2500 PICKUP 2WD
K2500 PICKUP 4WD
POSTAL CAB CHASSIS 2WD
R1500 SUBURBAN 2WD
SAFARI AWD (CARGO)
SAFARI AWD (PASSENGER)
SAFARI 2WD (CARGO)
SAFARI 2WD (PASSENGER)
SILHOUETTE 2WD
SONOMA PICKUP 2WD
SONOMA PICKUP 4WD
S10 BLAZER 2WD
S10 BLAZER 4WD
S10 PICKUP 2WD
S10 PICKUP 4WD
TRACKER CONVERTIBLE 2WD
TRACKER CONVERTIBLE 4WD
TRACKER 4WD
TRANS SPORT 2WD
V1500 BLAZER 4WD
V1500 JIMMY 4WD
V1500 SUBURBAN 4WD

Callaway Pas

CALLAWAY TWIN-TURBO
   CORVETTE

PAS-SYCLONE

1991 FOREIGN-MADE CARS

Chrysler

COLT
COLT VISTA
DB 132/DIABLO
LASER
MONACO
PREMIER
STEALTH
SUMMIT

TALON
TC BY MASERATI CONVERTIBLE
AD150 RAMCHARGER 2WD
AW150 RAMCHARGER 4WD
COLT VISTA 4WD
ROWER RAM 50 4WD
RAM 50 2WD

Ford

CAPRI
FESTIVA
JAGUAR XJ-S CONVERTIBLE

JAGUAR XJ-S COUPE
JAGUAR XJ6
VIRAGE SALOON

General Motors

ALLANTE
CENTURY
CENTURY WAGON
CUTLASS CALAIS
CUTLASS CIERA
CUTLASS CRUISER
FIREFLY
LEMANS

LOTUS ELAN
LOTUS ESPRIT TURBO
SAAB 900
SAAB 900 CONVERTIBLE
SAAB 9000
SKYLARK
SPRINT
STORM

BMW

M3
M5
318I CONVERTIBLE
318IS
325I CONVERTIBLE
325I/325IS
325IX

525I
535I
735I
735IL
750IL
850I

Daihatsu

CHARADE

ROCKY 4WD

Mercedes

190E2.3
190E2.6
300CE
300D 2.5 TURBO
300E
300E 2.6
300E-4MATIC

350SD TURBO
350SDL TURBO
420SEL
500SL
560SEC
560SEL

Fiat

MONDIAL T/CABRIOLET
SPIDER
TESTAROSSA

164
348 TB/TS

Honda

ACCORD
ACCORD WAGON
CIVIC
CIVIC CRX
CIVIC WAGON

CIVIC WAGON 4WD
INTEGRA
LEGEND
NSX
PRELUDE

Hyundai

EXCEL
SCOUPE

SONATA

Isuzu

IMPULSE
STYLUS
AMIGO 2WD
AMIGO 4WD

PICKUP 2WD
RODEO 2WD
RODEO 4WD
TROOPER

Nissan

AXXESS   ·
AXXESS AWD
G20
MAXIMA
M30

NX COUPE
Q45
Q45 FULL-ACTIVE SUSPENSION
SENTRA
STANZA

240SX	PATHFINDER 4WD
300ZX	TRUCK 2WD
300ZX 2 + 2	TRUCK 4WD
PATHFINDER 2WD	

Peugeot

405 SEDAN	505 STATION WAGON
405 SPORTS WAGON	

Porsche

911 CARRERA 4/2	928 S4
911 TURBO	944 S2

Rover

RANGE ROVER

Rolls-Royce

BENTLEY CONTINENTAL	CORNICHE III
BENTLEY EIGHT/MULSANNE S	SLIVER SPIRIT II/SILVER SPUR II
BENTLEY TURBO R	

Mitsubishi-Motor

ECLIPSE	3000 GT
GALANT	MONTERO
MIRAGE	TRUCK 2WD
PRECIS	TRUCK 4WD
SPACE WAGON	

Suzuki

METRO LSI CONVERTIBLE	SAMURAI 2WD
SWIFT	SIDEKICK HARDTOP 4WD
SWIFT GT	SIDEKICK SOFT-TOP 4WD
SAMURAI HARDTOP 4WD	SIDEKICK 2WD
SAMURAI SOFT-TOP 4WD	

Toyokogyo

MAZDA RX-7
MX-5 MIATA
323 PROTEGE 4X4
323/323 PROTEGE
626/MX-6

929
B2200/B2600I
B2600I 4X4
MPV
MPV 4X4

Toyota

CAMRY
CAMRY WAGON
CELICA
CELICA CONVERTIBLE
COROLLA
COROLLA ALL-TRAC WAGON
COROLLA WAGON
CRESSIDA
ES250
LS400
MR2

SUPRA
TERCEL
CAB/CHASSIS 2WD
LAND CRUISER WAGON 4WD
PREVIA
PREVIA ALL-TRAC
TRUCK 2WD
TRUCK 4WD
1-TON TRUCK 2WD
4-RUNNER 2WD
4-RUNNER 4WD

Volkswagen

CARBIOLET
CORRADO
COUPE QUATTRO
FOX
GOLF/GTI
GTI 16V
JETTA
JETTA GLI 16V
PASSAT
PASSAT WAGON
V8

100
100 QUATTRO
200
200 QUATTRO 20V
200 QUATTRO 20V WAGON
80 QUATTRO
80/90
90 QUATTRO 20V
VANAGON SYNCRO 4WD
VANAGON 2WD

Volvo

COUPE
240
240 WAGON
740
740 WAGON
940 GLE 16-VALVE

940 GLE 16-VALVE WAGON
940 SE
940 SE WAGON
940 TURBO
940 TURBO WAGON

Fuji

JUSTY
JUSTY 4WD
LEGACY
LEGACY TURBO
LEGACY WAGON
LEGACY WAGON 4WD
LEGACY 4WD

LEGACY 4WD TURBO
LOYALE
LOYALE WAGON
XT
XT 4WD
LOYALE WAGON 4WD
LOYALE 4WD

19

American Cars That Compete With Any in the World

American car manufacturers are striking back with an array of quality cars that exceed imports in quality and value. The only problem: most Americans don't know it.

OVERVIEW

Who doesn't know about America's car problems? Proud to be the world leaders during the 1950s and 1960s, American automobile manufacturers became fat, happy, and distracted during the 1970s and 1980s. Many wandered from their core business of building the kind of cars consumers most wanted. They wound up misinvesting money, buying everything from airplane manufacturers to data processing firms. When higher oil prices allowed the Japanese to get a foothold in this country by selling small, reliable cars, American firms were slow to respond. Instead of retooling and embracing new, more efficient manufacturing techniques, they stuck with outmoded styles and technologies. They then wasted valuable time pointing fingers at their Japanese rivals. The result: the Big Three lost $10 billion in 1991 alone as consumers searched for better quality and value.

But the good news is that desperate times have forced American automotive manufacturers to come to terms with their shortcomings. Make no doubt about it, there's a renaissance taking place in American car manufacturing. *Fortune* magazine has called it "The U.S. Car Comeback." It's being spurred by improved productivity and a commitment to quality never before seen in American car manufacturing. Surprisingly, a number of new models don't only meet, but exceed, the standards laid down by imports.

If you don't believe it, consider:

- Ford is now more cost-efficient than Toyota or Honda at making small four-cylinder cars, according to the Economic Strategy Institute, a private, Washington, D.C. research firm.

- American car manufacturers have improved productivity to such a degree that their manufacturing costs per vehicle are nearly the same as those of the Japanese, about $7,500 per car.

- In its first year of eligibility, Saturn vaulted to third on the J.D. Power & Associates customer satisfaction survey, beaten only by Lexus and Infiniti, both of which cost two to four times more than a Saturn.

- With the release of its new LH cars, Chrysler's sales surged dramatically during the third quarter of 1992, proving that an American car company could launch an important and impressive line that appeals to today's consumers.

But all that's secondary evidence. The proof is in the pudding. And the truth is that many American cars are just as good as imports and actually sell well outside the United States and the closed markets of Japan and other nations. What are our top cars? Here's a rundown.

- Cadillac STS. *Motor Trend's* 1992 Car of the Year, it's everything Lexus should be. Handsomely styled with a high-tech double overhead camshaft aluminum North Star engine in 1993 models, this is the car that has brought many aging baby boomers back to the American fold. It has not been out of patriotism, however: the Cadillac STS has all the feel and style of a German or Japanese touring car, but is priced at about $8,500 less.

- Saturn. This was General Motors' bold attempt to embrace Japanese management and production techniques. According to the motor press and the J.D. Power & Associates survey, the company has succeeded. Small and sporty, the car has been so popular that dealers don't have enough of them to sell. It's being promoted as the car of choice for first-time buyers, may of whom would never have considered an American car—before Saturn.

- Chrysler Concorde, Dodge Intrepid, and Eagle Vision (LH cars). A Hail Mary pass on the part of Chrysler designed to stave off utter destruction of the company. It's the first from-the-ground-up new model from Chrysler since 1980, and it's impressive. Its cab-forward design extends the passenger compartment over the front wheels. The rear wheels are extended to the back of the vehicle platform. The result: unprecedented interior passenger space and a more stable, comfortable ride. "The LH cars will have imports playing catch-up for the first time in fifteen years," fawns an automotive reviewer who has previewed the car.

- Jeep Grand Wagoneer. Redesigned in 1992, the Wagoneer is the ultimate yuppie sport utility, popular with city folk who want a little country in their urban lives. It's perfect for fox hunts or lugging the kids across town, and is among the best-riding sport utilities. Along with its cousin, the Jeep Cherokee, the Wagoneer is responsible for spawning the sport utility segment of the automotive industry. It's still the pick of the litter, with a quick-accelerating, 6-cylinder engine.

Why You Should Care

The automotive industry is arguably our country's most important. One out of seven American jobs is related to it. Cars account for 4.5 percent of our gross national product. For every 1,000 American cars sold, 150 jobs are created in our economy. Gus Stelzer, Mill Creek, Washington, in a letter to the editor of *Business Week*, writes:

"When are we going to realize that when a 100% American-made car priced to a dealer at $15,000 leaves a U.S. factory, it generates over $6,000 in tax revenues (and over $24,000, based on conservative ripple multiplier ratios), whereas a comparably priced import produces less than $400 with no ripple multiplier?...Every U.S. auto is better than every import because it contains features you can't get on any import—schools, crime prevention, roads, bridges, defense, health care, social security, real deficit reduction. American producers pay most of the taxes to support these and many other things we take for granted."

What You Can Do

If you're thinking about buying a new car, at least test-drive an American-made car. You will probably be surprised at how quickly American car manufacturers have closed the gap with their foreign competition. The EPA listing of domestic cars (listed in Chapter 18) provides the guidelines for which cars are made in America.

Also, encourage friends and relatives to test-drive an American-made car. The quality, in feel and handling, will be immediately apparent.

20

Recycle Your Car

*Want a quality car that won't cost you
much money or the country any jobs?
Try remanufacturing your automobile.*

OVERVIEW

If you go out to buy a new car, chances are one in three you
will wind up with an import. That's because Toyota, Mazda,
Audi, Volvo, and other foreign car manufacturers now command nearly one-third of the U.S. new-car market. Putting it
another way, one out of every three dollars spent on new cars in
this country goes to foreign workers and their families.

Why not keep that money here at home, along with those
jobs? There's a simple way to do it: you can remanufacture your
car.

It works something like this: take the typical four- or five-
year-old car in this country. It's paid off and probably still in
decent shape. You could trade it in, get a few thousand dollars
for it, and apply the money to buying a new car—and end up
with monthly payments of between $250 to $450.

Or, you could take that same car and systematically have its
major components—brakes, transmission, motor—rebuilt and
tuned up at any of the millions of American automotive service
businesses.

It's not a radical idea. The concept is being pioneered by
entrepreneurs across the country. In Philadelphia, for instance,
Motorworks, a chain of engine rebuilding businesses, is urging

78

consumers to trade in their engines instead of their cars when a head gasket fails.

Out west in Denver, Malcolm Bricklin, the genius behind the Bricklin automobile, is launching a new automotive business that takes used cars and restores them to "like-new" condition before they are resold.

Remanufacturing Makes Sense

Today's cars are better built than ever before. New polymer paints have vastly reduced body rust, increasing a car's life expectancy dramatically. Many of the chronic flaws that plagued cars years ago have been corrected. In fact, the average age of a car on the road today is 7.9 years, better than at any other time in history. After only four or five years of use, most cars still have a lot of life and value in them. All they probably need is some professional attention.

Why Remanufacturing Saves Jobs

Midas, Cottman, MAACO, AAMCO. These are all well-known names in the automobile aftermarket. They are also all American-owned businesses that employ American workers. So when you buy their products and services you can be reasonably sure your money goes to local workers—maybe even friends, family, and neighbors.

PRACTICAL STEPS

First, you have to determine if it's worth investing money in remanufacturing your car. Ask yourself, Has the car performed well until now? Does it need new tires, a new paint job, or other minor improvements?

Next, get a computer diagnostic performed on your car. Many service stations now own these machines. By simply hooking the computer to your car, a technician can perform a full diagnostic that examines the car's electrical and ignition systems, as well as its sophisticated computers. Cost of the report: $70 to $100.

Then, have a top-notch mechanic go over the car, both inside and out. What does it need and about how much will it cost? Expect to pay about $100 for the review.

Finally, make a list of everything the car needs. Call local body shops and service centers to determine the total costs of remanufacturing the vehicle.

The Costs

Surprisingly, you can save a ton of money by remanufacturing rather than trading in your car. Here's a breakdown of typical costs:

Rebuilt transmission	$900
New paint job and minor body work	900
New tires	300
New muffler	100
Shocks	150
Tune-up	70
Total	$2,420

To cover the costs, look into a home equity loan. The interest payments are deductible and the rates are typically lower than credit card rates or signature loans. A $3,000 home equity loan at 11 percent interest over thirty-six months costs about $100 per month. That's a lot more manageable than many new-car monthly payments!

Inside Tip

Buy Cooper Tires. They are made here in America. Also, tell mechanics that you want American-made parts. Most will comply if they are available.

21

Save America

Investing in American businesses and enterprises gives us the critical capital needed to buy manufacturing plants and equipment that put Americans to work.

OVERVIEW

What many Americans fail to understand about their own economy is that personal savings and investments are essential to productivity and job creation. Businesses need money—or capital—to build plants and upgrade equipment. So, those capital investments put people to work, while improving our country's ability to create quality consumer products.

Unfortunately, America is not a country of savers. While the Japanese and Germans enjoy a personal savings rate of 11.2 percent and 16 percent, respectively, Americans save a miserly 5.5 percent of their personal income. "One of the major problems affecting our nation's economy is the infamously low savings rate, which in turn brings low investment, low innovation, and low productivity," says Edward I. O'Brien, president of the Securities Industry Association.

The problem is exacerbated by the aging of our population. As more Americans advance through their prime savings ages of thirty-five to fifty-five, they miss the opportunity to pump important investment capital into the country's economy. Once they reach the other side of sixty, aging Americans become a draw against this country's capital base, using money from savings to finance their retirement.

Save America

Surprisingly, the problem isn't so much that Americans don't want to save. Rather, it's that they don't know how and haven't been conditioned to save. We're spenders, short and sweet. And more and more, the things we buy exchange our country's capital (the most precious of commodities) for quickly depreciating, foreign-made assets, everything from CD Walkmen to Lexus automobiles.

Americans must start saving more if they want to save their jobs, their standards of living, their dreams, hopes, and aspirations. We can no longer afford to finance our future through deficit spending and through the largess of others, primarily foreign investors, who are buying everything from Houston office towers to Hawaiian resorts.

What You Can Do

Invest American. Where should you put your money to get the best return and at the same time help create new American jobs?

As baby boomers sort through savings and investment decisions, they are arriving at the same conclusion their parents did: stocks are one of the few investment alternatives that offer the average person a good chance of keeping up with the growth of the economy and inflation. Based on the Standard and Poor's 500 index, the annualized total return (with dividends reinvested) on stocks since 1960 has been about 10 percent. That compares with a 6 percent annual return from Treasury bonds, 7 percent annual growth in home prices, and 5 percent annual overall inflation rate. Even after adjusting for inflation, a $1,000 investment in the Standard and Poor's 500 in 1960 would be worth $4,400 today.

Investing in American companies isn't as easy as it might first appear. Mutual funds, the savings vehicle of choice for millions of Americans, invest categorically, which is to say they direct their investment toward certain industries. Consequently, there is no guarantee that your mutual fund will invest in American-only companies.

There are some exceptions, however. Mutual funds that invest in utilities are de facto "American-only" funds because they invest in large electric, gas, and water utilities in this country. Consequently, when you invest in a utilities fund, you're likely to be pumping your money directly into American companies.

American-Only Funds. Americans are selective in choosing their causes. "Green" mutual funds, those that invest in supposedly environmentally friendly companies, have won favor, even though their bias might reduce returns. Americans were equally as committed to withdrawing their investments from companies that did business in South Africa to avoid supporting apartheid.

When it comes to investing strictly in American companies to help generate U.S. jobs, however, Americans have been surprisingly quiet. That has to end. We need more American-only mutual funds. Unfortunately, we know of only one. It is:

First Investors Made in the U.S.A. Fund
First Investors Corporation
10 Woodbridge Center Drive
Woodbridge, New Jersey 07095-1198
Denise Burns, investment manager
800-423-4026

The fund, which was just started in August 1992, is so new that it doesn't have much of a track record. But we like its investment criteria. According to the company, at least 65 percent of the fund's total assets will be invested in companies that employ at least two-thirds of their workers here, produce parts in America that constitute at least two-thirds of the value of the products sold by the company, or provide at least two-thirds of the value of their service within the United States.

According to the company's chief investment officer, Clark Wagner, the companies that fit the fund's profile are such firms as American Telephone & Telegraph, Wal-Mart Stores, General Mills, Rubbermaid, and Hershey Foods.

Dividend Reinvestment Plans. No matter how big or small your investment budget, there is one way to invest directly in American companies without paying the fees and commissions of a mutual fund. Dividend reinvestment plans allow individuals to buy single shares or even partial shares of a company directly, without a broker's commission. The dividend is then reinvested in the plan, allowing you to accumulate more shares of stocks.

Sources

1. Subscribe to *The Moneypaper*, an investment newsletter through which you can buy single shares of many different companies. Once you own the share, you can enroll in the dividend reinvestment plan and thereafter buy small amounts of shares directly from the company. Minimum amounts vary. For example, Quaker Oats will accept investments as small as $10 once you are in the plan.
For information, write:
    The Moneypaper
    1010 Mamaroneck Avenue
    Mamaroneck, New York 10543
    914-381-5400
    One-year subscription: $72
2. Join the National Association of Investors Corporation (NAIC). Like *The Moneypaper*, NAIC assists investors in buying their initial share of stock, from which they can then enroll in the dividend reinvestment plan and make additional investments. For information, write or call:
    NAIC
    1515 East Eleven Mile Road
    Royal Oak, Michigan 48067
    313-543-0612
    Cost to join: $32

Once you're in, it's up to you to find out whether the company you're investing in is American or not. How can you tell?
- Read its annual report.
- Is it an American company doing business, selling product, and employing people in the United States?
- Who are the majority stockholders? Americans? Foreign corporations, etc.?
- Where are its major production facilities: Toledo or Tokyo?

Mastering the Environment for Jobs

22

Recycle for American Jobs

Recycle your garbage not just into new products,
but into new jobs for Americans.

OVERVIEW

The equation is so simple: the more material we recycle, the more Americans we put to work. Why? Recycling is a labor-intensive process that requires hands-on employees every step of the way. And better yet, it's a growth industry. According to a Roper Organization poll, preserving the environment is the fastest-growing concern among Americans. Look at some of the figures.

- The Environmental Protection Agency says that 17 percent of America's trash now gets recycled, and that by 1995 the figure will rise to 25 percent.

- The Council for Solid Waste reports that in 1990, 532 million pounds of plastic packaging were recycled, a 51 percent increase from 1989.

- The Aluminum Association says nearly forty-four billion aluminum beverage cans were recycled in 1990, earning the recycling industry $2 million a day.

- The amount of money collectively spent by all fifty states on recycling in 1992 will increase by almost 50 percent in 1993, according to *Waste Age* magazine.

When organizations spend money, they create jobs, period. And you can make sure that industry and municipalities continue to spend money on recycling by making sure you contribute to the recycling stream. Yes, your trash is part of the solution, environmentally and economically.

A Brief Case Study

Browning Ferris Industries (BFI), a $3.1 billion publicly held corporation, demonstrates the impact recycling can have on job creation. According to Charles Oyler, one of the company's recycling development managers, approximately 25 percent of BFI's 26,000 employees nationwide owe their jobs to the recycling movement in the United States.

"Recycling is a very labor-intensive process," says Oyler. "At one facility we recycle one hundred forty tons of material daily. That kind of volume requires forty employees for two shifts. And we need additional haulers, sorters, and drivers."

Oyler points out that recycling also creates white-collar jobs. "There is a growing need for consultants who advise schools, communities, and corporations on recycling programs. Also, marketing and sales representatives must be out in the field to sell the recycled goods to paper mills, glass mills, and aluminum manufacturing companies."

Oyler points out that many companies are just now beginning to realize profits from their recycling operations. "There are high costs associated with the training and education of employees and the awareness programs for communities and for customers." And, he says, that doesn't begin to touch the investment in equipment, including trucks, conveyor belts, extruders, and warehouses. So, not only does BFI create jobs directly through its recycling operations, but the company's considerable capital investments have a ripple effect throughout the economy.

"We knew we had to make the investment," says Oyler, "because that's where the future lies. Presently, recycling accounts for about ten percent of our revenues, but we know this will grow tremendously in the coming years. There's no choice. Recycling makes good environmental sense and it makes good business sense."

What You Can Do

Recycle for American jobs. To do this, we need to increase the volume of material we recycle. And so, we need every American to participate in recycling programs.

• Start a recycling center at home. Pick up the telephone, call your town or city manager, and find out what recycling programs exist in your town and what you need to do to participate. Some communities are required by law to sort and recycle newspapers, glass, plastics, and hazardous waste material. Other communities encourage recycling, but cannot afford the costs of picking up the material.

• If your community does not have recycling, contact your township or county commission and find out where you can take your recyclable materials.

• Start a recycling program at work, school, church, or any club or organization to which you belong.

• Learn how to recycle. When you do it correctly, you make the industry more profitable and attractive for additional investment. For example, crushing aluminum or plastic containers cuts down on cubic volume, which in turn reduces transportation costs. You can learn how to recycle better by calling Keep America Beautiful and asking for information on recycling. In addition, the organization can teach you how to get a recycling charter in your city or town. Write to:

Keep America Beautiful
9 West Broad Street
Stamford, Connecticut 06902
203-323-8987

Or call the EPA (202-260-2090) and ask for its *Consumer's Handbook for Reducing Solid Waste,* as well as other packets. Write to:

Office of Solid Waste
EPA
401 M Street SW
Washington, D.C. 20460

Compounding Your Impact

Recycle glass. More than eleven *billion* glass containers were imported into the United States during 1990. According to the Glass Manufacturers Institute, this imported glass is a problem. First, using glass containers that have been manufactured overseas means taking jobs away from glassmakers here. Second, American glass manufacturers must bear all the cost and responsibility for the recycling of foreign glass that ends up here. This makes them less competitive, less profitable, and less likely to expand and hire more people.

23

Strike Back at the Earth's Worst Polluters

Many products from emerging countries are less expensive.
But then again, those prices don't include
environmental compliance.

OVERVIEW

Here in America, we have accepted the fact that environmental destruction will be felt for generations and that we have a moral obligation to leave a living, breathing planet to our children and to their children.

In many foreign nations, however, this thinking does not apply. As an environmental reporter for the *Wall Street Journal* tells it, "After you get past the top five or six industrial nations, countries either plow waste into the earth, pump it into the air, or throw it down the sink."

The irony is that while many Americans are passionate about environmental issues, they willingly or thoughtlessly buy products from nations with heinous environmental records, simply to save a few pennies.

The American track record on the environment may not be perfect, but the United States does have some of the strictest environmental regulations in the world. And the price of our products reflects all of the costs, including the environmental ones, of producing, transporting, consuming, and disposing of goods and services.

The bottom line? When you buy products from certain countries, you are subsidizing the systematic destruction of the earth.

So if you haven't been able to find a compelling argument to buy American products, try this one: the purchase of American goods sends a message that consumers value environmental issues and are willing to pay the price to protect the earth.

Where It Hurts the Most

A World Health Organization and United Nations report, *Urban Air Pollution in Megacities of the World*, lists the ten most polluted areas in terms of suspended particulate matter from domestic fires, power generation, and industry. These cities are:

1. Mexico City, Mexico
2. Bangkok, Thailand
3. Beijing, China
4. Bombay, India
5. Jakarta, Indonesia
6. Seoul, Korea
7. Karachi, Pakistan
8. Delhi, India
9. Calcutta, India
10. Cairo, Egypt

To meet the burgeoning demand from vast Western markets, developing countries will step up production by using cheap and available energy sources, such as carbon dioxide-laden, low-grade coal.

The report goes on to say that in Latin America, some two million children suffer from chronic coughs as a result of breathing urban air pollution and that in Third World nations, some fourteen million children under age five will die annually of environmentally related diseases. It adds that 66 percent of these deaths could have been prevented by using simple, environmentally sound processes in every area of daily life.

What You Can Do

Don't buy products from countries with poor environmental records. As a consumer, you vote with your pocketbook; as an environmentalist, you use the same tool. When we stem the demand for products that come from recklessly polluting nations, we challenge them to meet or beat our own environmental standards. When they respond, and the trading field between us evens, our products become more price-competitive. We sell and produce more and more, and Americans are put to work. To achieve this leveling effect, here are five simple things you can do.

- Read the labels. Even though we searched high and low, we could not find a list of the worst polluting nations on earth. The United Nations, the World Health Organization, and other international agencies that compile statistics, are reluctant to sanction nations on a wholesale basis. The World Health Organization did however offer us the list (opposite) of the most polluted cities on earth. And we submit that the countries where these cities are located cannot be far behind in their environmental record. So use our list as a starting point for identifying countries whose products should be avoided on the basis of environmental carelessness. And, when you read authoritative news stories about other nations that are recklessly polluting, add them to your list of countries whose products you should avoid.

- To find a list of embassies in the metropolitan Washington D.C. area, get the *Diplomatic List*, sometimes referred to as the blue book. To get a list of all embassies in the United States, you'll need to get a book titled *Foreign Consular Offices*. The books cost $6.00 each and you can get them at any United States Government Bookstore. If you don't have one of these bookstores nearby, you can get these publications by mailing a check to the Superintendent of Documents, U.S. Government Bookstores, Washington, D.C. 20402. By the way, the blue book has a companion publication called *Employees of Diplomatic Missions*, which lists the personnel of the Washington, D.C. area embassies. The volume is also $6.00 and can be gotten through federal government bookstores.

- Join an environmental group, and actively support its cause. In addition, urge it to expand its sphere of influence and operations to other polluting nations. See Chapter 25 for a list of the most influential environmental groups in the United States.

• Write a member of Congress. Tell him or her you believe the environmental policies of the nations listed above, as well as those of many others, not only endanger future generations, but also take away American jobs. Tell your Congressperson you believe that most-favored-nation status should be tied to a country's environmental record. See Chapter 4 on how to deliver a letter to your legislator, with punch.

24

Saving Jobs by
Saving Energy

*The real culprit in America's trade imbalance
isn't cars, computers, or microchips, it's
imported oil. The sheer magnitude of our
dependence on foreign oil sucks trillions of
dollars and millions of jobs out of our economy.*

OVERVIEW

Oh, that nasty thing called the trade deficit. It looms out these as something for economists to fuss about, but doesn't mean much to the average American. Why should we care if this company imports more than it exports? What difference does it make if dollars flow out of our country faster than they flow in?

It makes a vital difference. The U.S. trade deficit, which topped $73 billion in the third quarter of 1992, serves as an EKG of our economic pulse. It tells us whether Americans are making the products the world's consumers want and lets us know how well we're doing as workers in the global economy.

Well, we're not faring too well. Our economy is hemorrhaging money, sending it off to foreigners so they can build plants and improve equipment, so they can put their people to work, at the sacrifice of our standard of living.

What accounts for this huge gap? Much of it—nearly half if it when measured in merchandise—is due to imported oil.

95

The United States is hooked on foreign sources of oil, and the addiction is getting worse. In 1985, we imported about 27 percent of all the oil we used, which was troubling. By 1989, that number had jumped to 46 percent. Within the next two decades, 61 percent of every gallon of gas and every tank of home heating oil we use will come from distant shores, mainly the unstable Middle East.

What You Can Do

We need to save energy if we are to slash the trade deficit and keep our money at home to create jobs. Here's what you can do:

Cars

1. When buying a new car, make fuel efficiency a prime concern. Window stickers are generally accurate, but you can also obtain free from all new-car dealers *The Gas Mileage Guide*, which compares the mileage rates of vehicles within the same class.

By choosing models that obtain fuel economies of just one more mile per gallon than the average for each vehicle class, consumers could save more than $400 in fuel costs over the life of the vehicle.

2. Address your transportation needs as objectively as possible. If you need the car predominantly for highway driving, opt for an automatic transmission and cruise control. City drivers would best conserve fuel with a manual transmission.

If you rarely have passengers in your vehicle, select lighter cars with smaller engines. If you live in a predominantly warm climate, choose vehicles with lighter exterior and interior colors. (Light hues reduce heat buildup and decrease the need for air-conditioning.) Cold-climate dwellers may find that flow-through ventilation systems may eliminate the need for air conditioning.

3. Observe speed limits and reduce highway speeds. The average U.S. driver exceeds the speed limit by approximately five miles per hour. For every one mile per hour above 55 mph, the average vehicle loses almost 2 percent in fuel economy. If

highway speed limits were observed across the nation, almost four million gallons of gasoline per day could be saved.

4. Employ energy-efficient driving techniques. Idling can kill fuel efficiency. If 145 million passenger vehicles idle for five minutes a day, this country wastes four million gallons of gasoline without going anywhere. So avoid drive-in banks and drive-through fast-food restaurants. And use the right-on-red option whenever possible.

5. Know your route. Trip planning may be your most important fuel saver. Listen to traffic reports and investigate alternative routes when traffic is backed up.

6. Don't buy higher-octane gasoline than your car needs. More crude oil is needed to refine higher-octane gasolines. Purchase the gasoline that the auto manufacturer suggests. The same advice goes for motor oils. The lowest possible viscosity oil is best for fuel economy.

7. Maintain tire pressure at recommended levels.

At Home

1. Protect your home from outside heat and cold. Use draft-proof windows and doors and eliminate other air leaks. Caulk and weather-strip existing doors and windows. Draft-free houses can save up to 10 percent on energy costs.

If every gas-heated home were properly caulked and weather-stripped, we'd save enough natural gas each year to heat about four million homes.

2. Insulate. A well-insulated home can reduce the load on heating and cooling equipment by as much as 20 to 30 percent.

Don't waste precious heated or cooled air, whether you pay for it yourself or your landlord pays for it. Don't turn on the heat until you have to. On cool evenings, wear warmer clothes. Close off unoccupied rooms and shut their heat or air-conditioning vents.

3. Lower thermostats to 65 degrees during the day and 60 degrees at night during cold months and 78 degrees in warmer temperatures.

If every household in the United States lowered its average

heating temperature six degrees over a twenty-four-hour period, we would save more than 570,000 barrels of oil per day.

If every household raised air-conditioning temperatures six degrees, we'd save the equivalent of 190,000 barrels of oil every day.

4. Have your oil furnace serviced at least once a year.

5. Consider a heat pump system. It can cut your use of electricity for heating by 30 percent to 40 percent.

6. Heating water accounts for about 15 percent of all the energy in our homes. So make sure to:

• Repair leaky faucets promptly.
• Do as much household cleaning as possible with cold water.
• Insulate your hot water storage tank and piping.
• Install low-flow shower heads.

A setting of 120 degrees can provide adequate hot water for most families. Most water heaters are set for 140 degrees or higher.

Reducing water temperature to 120 degrees could save more than 18 percent of the energy used.

7. Use water efficiently.

• Turn on the dishwasher only when there is a full load of dirty dishes.
• Wash laundry in either warm or cold water.
• Keep the lint screen in your dryer clean. This will cut down on the amount of time needed to dry laundry.
• Take showers rather than baths. This could cut in half the amount of water needed.

8. Don't use more light than you need. About 15 percent of the electricity we use in our homes goes into lighting.

• Use lamps with three-way switches.
• Install dimmers with high-low switches.

9. Investigate solar energy. Solar energy heating is not for everyone, but it might save energy if you have the right climate and building site and ample interior space to hold solar storage tanks.

Sources

Write:

The Department of Energy Conservation and Energy
Inquiry and Referral Service (CAREIRS)
P.O. Box 890
Silver Springs, Maryland 20907
800-523-2929

Department of Energy National Appropriate
Technology Assistance Service (NATAS)
P.O. Box 2525
Butte, Montana 59702-2525
800-428-2525 (or 800-428-1718 in Montana)

25

The Greening of America Could Produce Your Next Paycheck

By supporting environmental causes, you can help create American jobs.

OVERVIEW

So you want to protest acid rain but worry it will cost American jobs? Stop worrying. There's ample evidence that environmental regulation and compliance has actually spurred economic activity and jobs in this country.

How can that be? Simple. When businesses have to invest in equipment and technology to clean up their acts, other businesses have to manufacture the products and deliver the services to accomplish that goal.

The environment is big business, already generating more than $200 billion a year for the businesses engaged in cleaning up industry.

And it's a business in which America leads. Because we were among the first industrialized nations to address the problem, our businesses were among the first to develop the technologies and equipment needed to scrub smoke as it leaves a chimney or clean water as it is discharged from a factory.

So concern for the environment creates jobs! There's no conflict here.

Facts and Figures

A study by Stephen M. Meyer, a political science professor at M.I.T., shows that the states with the strongest economies are also the ones with the most stringent environmental regulation. His study reaches these conclusions:

1. For states that enacted strong environmental policies, economic growth was more than twice that of states with weak policies.

2. The majority of states that mandate stringent environmental controls showed the highest growth in employment, while states where environmental regulation was a low priority showed the weakest employment growth. The average employment growth rate was 45 percent greater in the environmentally strong states than it was in the weak ones.

3. Growth in construction was better in tightly regulated states than it was in loosely regulated ones. In fact, environmentally weak states actually posted a 1.4 percent decline in construction employment.

4. Labor productivity fared better in the environmentally strong states. Growth in productivity of the stronger states was approximately twice that of growth in the weaker ones.

America's Future in Environmental Industries

According to San Francisco-based investment banking powerhouse Robertson, Stephens & Co., environmental technologies will continue to grow here, thanks in large measure to the Clean Air Act and its amendments. The following sectors are expected to achieve the greatest growth.

1. Acid rain reduction technology. Still in its infancy, applications for this technology should generate $10 to $12 billion in revenues by the end of the decade.

2. Instrumentation and emission monitors. To date, the bulk of this market has been made up of utility companies, but aggressive new legislation will require the installation of monitoring equipment on cement, chemical, and waste-to-energy smokestacks. Currently a $100 to $150 million industry,

instrumentation and emission control is expected to grow some 50 to 70 percent per year.

3. Catalytic converters for cars, trucks, and other vehicles, already a $6 to $8 billion industry, is expected to grow, up to 10 percent annually.

And it's not just high technology that creates jobs. For example, the Utility Contractors Association reports that every $1 billion spent on water and sewer improvement and installation projects generates between 34,200 and 57,400 jobs.

Japan's Got the Idea

Japan sees pollution control as its next great industry and is mounting an "ecoindustrial" revolution. What's involved? A government blueprint for the next *one hundred years*, called New Earth 21, designed to convert the world's worst polluting industries to a new generation of clean technologies. And this plan is already under way, with dozens of companies at work making solar energy affordable for household use, perfecting wind turbines, and attacking global warming with new strains of carbon dioxide-devouring algae. At the Earth Summit in Rio de Janeiro, Japan pledged some $7 billion in environmental aid for developing nations, far more than any other country present. But Japan has more than saving the earth on its mind. As Japanese congressman Kazuo Aichi said when interviewed by ABC-TV's Ned Potter, "If we can start the ecoindustrial revolution, there will be a lot of chance for business."

What You Can Do

Create American jobs by supporting environmentalism.

Join local and national environmental groups. By doing so, you help keep the pressure on the president and on Congress to pass the kind of laws that create more jobs. Here are some of the most active groups in the United States that you can join and support:

Center for Marine
    Conservation
1725 DeSales Street NW
Washington, D.C. 20036

Citizen's Clearinghouse for
    Hazardous Waste
P.O. Box 926
Arlington, Virginia 22216

Citizens for a Better
Environment
33 East Congress
Suite 523
Chicago, Illinois 60605

Earth Island Institute
300 Broadway, Suite 28
San Francisco, California
94133

Environmental Action
1525 New Hampshire NW
Washington, D.C. 20036

Environmental Defense Fund
1616 P Street NW
Washington, D.C. 20036

Environmental Policy
Institute
218 D Street SE
Washington, D.C. 20003

Greenhouse Crisis
Foundation
1130 17th Street NW
Washington, D.C. 20036

Greenpeace
1436 U Street NW
Washington, D.C. 20009

National Audubon Society
801 Pennsylvania Avenue SE
Washington, D.C. 20003

National Coalition Against
the Misuse of Pesticides
530 Seventh Street SE
Washington, D.C. 20003

National Resources Defense
Council
40 West 20th Street
New York, New York 10011

National Wildlife Federation
1412 16th Street NW
Washington, D.C. 20036

The Nature Conservancy
1815 North Lynn Street
Arlington, Virginia 22209

North Wildlife Fund
1250 24th Street NW
Washington, D.C. 20037

Oceanic Society
218 D Street SE
Washington, D.C. 20003

Rainforest Action Network
300 Broadway
San Francisco, California
94113

Renew America
1400 16th Street NW
Washington, D.C. 20036

Rocky Mountain Institute
1739 Snowmass Creek Road
Snowmass, Colorado 81654

Sierra Club
730 Polk Street
San Francisco, California
94009

Wilderness Society
1400 I Street NW
Washington, D.C. 20006

World Resources Institute
1735 New York Avenue NW
Washington, D.C. 20006

Worldwatch Institute
1776 Massachusetts Avenue
NW
Washington, D.C. 20036

Write to your elected representatives and tell them that you support strong, restrictive environmental legislation. Tell them that not only does this help preserve the earth's natural resources for future generations, but that it also creates vital jobs here in America. In addition, tell them that you support government initiatives to maintain America's lead in environmental industries.

Attend public utility commissions meetings. There, voice your support for any proposed regulation of local utilities, and voice your opposition to attempts to circumvent regulation.

People, Places, and Products to Avoid in Your Fight to Save American Jobs

26

What Bo Doesn't Know

*If the image and mystique of American
athletes is good enough to sell products,
why aren't American workers good enough to make them?*

OVERVIEW

You've got to tip your hat to Michael Jordan and Bo Jackson. Like many sports greats, they've used their success on the playing courts and fields to sell some of the most popular and expensive sportswear in the world, including Nike and Reebok sneakers. That's the American way.

What doesn't follow the American way, though, is when the companies behind these products turn their backs on American workers. Although Nike and Reebok each spend more than $75 million a year to advertise their products using American athletes as their primary lure, neither one produces their high-end sneakers in this country. When pressed to explain why, spokespeople for Nike claim that it's impossible to pay high American wages and still turn a profit on their shoes, some of which sell for as much as $150 a pair.

Yet other athletic shoe manufacturers manage to successfully produce their products in the U.S. Saucony manufacturers its training shoes in Bangor, Maine, and New Balance makes them at four plants around the country.

Ironically, two of New Balance's plants are located in job-scarce urban areas, where sneaker buyers favor Nike and Reebok. One plant, in Lawrence, Massachusetts, stands among 500 abandoned buildings. Yet New Balance has not abandoned

107

the area's people. Some 180 workers turn out shoes at the company's factory on South Union Street.

According to New Balance chairman James Davis, the high-wage argument used by Nike simply doesn't carry weight. Davis contends that while American workers are paid much higher wages than those in China or Sri Lanka ($8 to $10 an hour, compared to $1 to $2 a day), labor costs represent only 15 percent of New Balance's total costs. That's because, Mr. Davis contends, his American workers are twice as productive as overseas labor.

What You Can Do

The Made in the USA Foundation has mounted an aggressive protect against Nike for producing its shoes outside the United States. Nike counters that while its shoes are made by foreigners, its apparel line is manufactured in this country and parts of Nike Air sneakers are also made here. Those explanations haven't convinced the Foundation. It maintains that Nike, an immensely profitable company, has simply abandoned U.S. workers, rubbing our noses in it every time it uses an American athlete to win worldwide markets for its products.

To protest Nike's stand on American jobs the Foundation recommends that you send your old, smelly sneakers to:
Philip Knight, Chairman
Nike
1 Bowerman Drive
Beaverton, Oregon 97005

And how about Michael Jordan and Bo Jackson? Both athletes are sensitive to the plight of inner-city minorities and the need to create opportunities in these pockets of poverty. You should urge both athletes to take an active role in lobbying Nike and Reebok to establish shoe-manufacturing facilities in U.S. cities.

Write to Michael Jordan c/o:
Chicago Bulls
980 North Michigan Avenue
Suite 1600
Chicago, Illinois 60611

Write to Bo Jackson c/o:

Chicago White Sox
333 West 35th Street
Chicago, Illinois 60616

A final thought

Shoe manufacturers aren't the only ones who use American cachet to sell products made by foreigners. The Smithsonian Institution recently contracted to have four well-known American quilt patterns made in China for sale in the United States via catalogs and stores. Speak out to manufacturers and any organizations that use our image or history to sell foreign-made goods.

27

Don't Support Exploited Labor

Slave labor helps some countries export products cheaply.
When we support it, we undermine human rights and
deny our own people jobs.

OVERVIEW

Cheap labor that steals American jobs is bad enough. But when a country uses slave labor to manufacture products for less than we can make them here, it's a downright crime.

Yet China has been accused of doing just that in manufacturing a vast array of products that are finding their way to Western markets. That has to stop. If we're to save American jobs, we've got to even the playing field and put our workers on the same footing with their foreign counterparts.

China: A Huge and Growing U.S. Supplier

In sheer size, China is a formidable economic power, with over one billion potential workers. So it's little wonder the country can produce some products at a fraction of the cost we can here.

Now we're learning that China has another advantage in winning trade through low-cost manufacturing. It's using imprisoned workers—in violation of human rights sanctions—to make some of its products.

The Smoking Gun

Suspicion that prison labor is used in China has always run high. Yet evidence was always lacking. But in 1991, the publication *Asia Watch*, a division of Human Rights Watch, produced undisputable evidence: articles from a "restricted circulation" publication, titled *Theoretical Studies in Labor Reform and Labor Reeducation*, that describes in detail the use of forced prison labor to produce goods for the West.

The articles, according to *Asia Watch*, are all written by prison officials and labor reform bureaucrats, and make it clear that forced labor is not an ad-hoc occurrence, but a central government policy.

In many articles, the authors boast of the advantages of prison labor. One passage reads:

A large number of prisoners have become commodity producers. They are cheap and concentrated. They produce labor-intensive products, and this accords with the discretion of transfer on the international market...

And what does this prison population face? Some of the grimmest working conditions on the face of the earth, according to *Asia Watch*. Many tasks are dangerous. Medical services range from rudimentary to nonexistent. Food rations are often cut as a means of discipline or punishment for not meeting production quotas. And in some prisons a "strict regime" is often meted out to political prisoners, which consists of solitary confinement and the "four cessations"—no visits, no personal money, no letters, no leisure activities. In most cases the political prisoners never leave their cells, but perform their mind-numbing production hour after hour, day after day.

Our Government's Position

The Tariff Act of 1930 prevents the entry of goods into the United States manufactured in whole or part by prison or forced labor. To date there has been but a single application of the law. That was in 1951, when Soviet crabmeat was banned from importation for ten years after it was judged to have been produced by prison labor. But the U.S. government seems reluctant to impose sanctions against a current trading partner, and one that could someday become the world's largest economy. Our government does not attempt to deny the existence of prison labor, but claims there is no proof that imported Chinese goods have been produced by prison or forced labor. The result? China has been granted Most Favored Nation status, or what amounts to unrestricted access to our markets, since 1980.

What You Can Do

Stop buying Chinese goods. As consumers, we can take a moral stand against the use of slave labor by not buying Chinese-made products. In turn, that will put more dollars in the hands of U.S. producers, who rely on American workers to make products under humane conditions.

Write to your elected representatives and tell them to vote against the granting of Most Favored Nation status for China. MFN status is granted as a matter of course to free enterprise countries, but relies on an annual presidential waiver of the 1974 Trade Act for Communist nations. Congress has the power to veto this waiver and votes on it every year. You have the power to decide how Congress votes on this important question.

Write to retailers who carry a preponderance of Chinese-made products and express your disapproval. Products commonly exported to the United States from China: toys, footwear, knit and nonknit apparel, leather goods, machinery and parts, petroleum, plastics, and furniture.

A Final Thought

Remember, economic sanctions proved effective against South Africa, Zimbabwe, and the former Soviet Union. The actions we recommend are not designed to be punitive, but to lure China toward reform so that she may be a genuine and productive member of the world economy—and help create American jobs.

28

Buy America Programs: The Good, the Bad & the Ugly

When retailers make claims that their merchandise is all-American, send up a red flag.

OVERVIEW

Sure buying American is tough. And sometimes you'll get fooled. But that doesn't mean you should stop trying.

In certain instances, we must accept that some retailers and businesses will deceptively wrap themselves in the American flag, regardless of whether or not their products are American-made and generate American jobs. The reality is that if you want to buy American goods, you've got to be a bit skeptical and a little forgiving.

A Brief Case Study

The late Sam Walton, founder of Wal-Mart, America's largest retailer, hit upon a great idea in 1985. His Buy America campaign, which focused on highlighting domestic goods in stores and a commitment to buying goods from American manufacturers, was good for the country and good for Wal-Mart.

And it also helped other U.S. companies. Mr. Coffee, for instance, was able to convert four of its products from overseas to domestic production. Fieldcrest Cannon got the order for 12-pack washcloths that Wal-Mart used to buy from Japan. And

Capital Mercury Shirt Co. brought back all of its overseas production. Each of these events created American jobs, and for every one of them we owe a debt of gratitude to Wal-Mart and its innovative thinking. Unfortunately for Wal-Mart, the campaign suffered a serious setback at the close of 1992, embroiling the company in a cloud of controversy. NBC's investigative news program "Dateline NBC" conducted an intensive investigation into Wal-Mart's Buy America program and found it wanting in several areas.

"NBC Dateline" found garments in Wal-Mart stores that hung underneath signs reading "Made in the USA" whose labels revealed they were made in Bangladesh.

When "Dateline" traveled to the Bangladeshi factories that made those Wal-Mart products, it reportedly found sweatshop conditions and child labor. The reporters dug deeper and discovered Wal-Mart ties to companies engaged in illegally smuggling foreign goods into this country. They also uncovered that Wal-Mart stopped buying products from American manufacturers when the company landed slightly lower prices from foreign manufacturers.

Wal-Mart's president and chief executive officer, David Glass, publicly apologized to customers that merchandise in some stores had been marked "Made in the USA" even though the labels on each garment identified them as imported.

Accident or no, the damage had already been done. In the minds of many consumers, special programs to encourage American buying were labeled a sham.

What You Can Do

1. **Be skeptical.** Realize that among other things, mistakes can be made. Look for the promotions, sure, but read the labels as well.

2. **If you find merchandise incorrectly marked, see the manager.** Tell him or her about the situation and ask where the real American goods are.

3. **Don't let one example or situation turn you off to Buy America programs.** Let the managers at the places you shop

know that such a program would get—or has, if it's already in place—your full support.

4. Adjust your attitude. Recognize that you might have to pay more for American products. Is that because American workers are unproductive and demand uncompetitive wages? Absolutely not. Built into the cost of every American-made product is a piece of the country's agenda, which among other things embodies:

> Social security
> Environmental regulations
> Safety regulations
> Antidiscrimination legislation
> Unemployment insurance
> Child labor laws

So when you buy inexpensively produced foreign goods, from places where there may be no regard for the environment or the sanctity of childhood, you're not necessarily saying you don't want these things, but you are saying that you are not willing to pay for them.

29

Buy From Our Partners, Not Our Parasites

Buying some foreign products can actually create jobs. The trick is to know which countries do the best job in reciprocating trade with us.

OVERVIEW

Sound the "Buy American" cry too often or too loud, and you run the risk of being tagged petty, or just plain stupid. "We live in a global economy," the critics will argue. "So when you buy foreign products, you raise their standard of living, so that they can buy more of ours."

Well, that sounds great in theory. And in fact, some countries, like Japan, do a very convincing job in arguing for free trade. But the irony is that some of the most vocal free-traders, such as Japan and her high-priced lobbyists, do not practice what they preach. They want to sell in this country; they want Americans to buy their products. But that door only swings one way. Because they do not want American products in their markets or on their shelves.

Free trade is critical to our economic development. But it only works when everyone is playing by the same rules. Some of our trading partners do play by the rules, and it benefits us both. Others? With them it's a one-way street.

The Problem in Practice

Let's look at Japan. Sure they buy American products, and that's important, but they sell much, much more than they buy.

116

In fact, in many industries where Japan has a substantial presence in the United States, we can't even get a foothold in Japan. A September 7, 1992 study by *Fortune* magazine ranked the "levelness" of Japan's playing field on a few critical trade issues. When you read it, you'll see why Japan made our list of trading parasites.

Consumer Items: A moderately steep playing field. *Why?* Penetrating Japan's convoluted distribution system is difficult. *Difficulties they face in the United States*: None for electronics or other products, voluntary agreements for cars and trucks.

Patent Protection: A moderately steep playing field. *Why?* Long delays in receiving patents, during which time Japanese firms can pore over the applications. *Difficulties they face in the United States*: A business culture where lawsuits for patent infringements are more common than in Japan.

Automobile Parts: A steep playing field. *Why?* Reluctance of Japanese automakers to switch from traditional suppliers, with many bound by a cultural phenomenon called *keiretsu* that excludes outsiders. *Difficulties they face in the United States:* None.

Direct Investment: A steep playing field. *Why?* Cross-ownership of many Japanese companies keeps outsiders from buying control of large firms. *Difficulties they face in the United States*: None, except where law prohibits, such as in defense industries.

Construction: A very steep playing field. *Why?* Collusion among Japanese bidders. *Difficulties they face in the United States*: None.

Soda Ash: A very steep playing field. *Why?* Industrial customers are persuaded by its domestic producers not to buy less expensive American product. *Difficulties they face in the United States*: None. Japanese companies do export to the United States.

Flat Glass: The playing field is practically vertical. *Why?* Pressure by Japanese glassmaking cartel on construction industry and other users restricts U.S. imports to less than 0.5 percent of the market.

Difficulties they face in the United States: None. Japanese have built U.S. plants and command 10 percent of the market.

What does it all mean? A trade deficit with Japan of staggering proportion: in 1991, *$43.4 billion.*

What You Can Do

Buy from countries that are our partners, not our parasites. By supporting those with open markets, you ensure that we grow wealthy and create jobs together.

A Ranking of Deficit and Surplus Nations

When a country continually sells more here than they buy (a trade surplus for them, and a trade deficit for us), it becomes a draw on our economy, sucking away American jobs. Here are the countries that continually sold more than they bought (figures from 1991) and that accordingly earn membership in our Parasites Club.

Country	Surplus in Billions
Japan	$43.4
China	12.7
Taiwan	9.8
Canada	6.0
Germany	4.9
Nigeria	4.5
Saudi Arabia	4.4
Venezuela	3.5
Italy	3.2
Thailand	2.4

One of the worst offenders? Thailand. While American exports have surged in the last few years, causing the trade deficit of even the nine others mentioned above to narrow, Thailand's has grown each year, from just $579 million in 1985 to more than $2 billion in 1991.

On the other hand, some countries run trade surpluses. That is, they buy more from us than they sell to us. They get to join our Partners Club.

Country	Surplus in Billions
Netherlands	$8.7
Belgium/Luxembourg	6.7
Australia	4.4
United Kingdom	3.5
Spain	2.6
Egypt	2.5
Mexico	2.0
France	2.0
Turkey	1.4

What Is a Trade Barrier?

The Office of the U.S. Trade Representative, in its 1992 annual report to Congress and the president, classifies trade barriers under eight different categories. They are:

- Import policies such as quantitative restrictions or charges or import licensing.

- Unnecessarily restrictive standards, testing, labeling, and certification.

- Government procurement policies, such as "Buy National" or closed bidding.

- Export subsidies.

- Absence of intellectual property protection for patents, trademarks, and copyrights.

- Services barriers, such as regulation of data flow or restrictions on the use of foreign data processing.

- Investment barriers.

- Other barriers.

A Final Thought

When foreign trade is mentioned, you hear the words "a billion dollars" quite frequently. But what does it mean? In terms of jobs, about 2,000. That's right. Every billion dollars in exported goods and services generates about 2,000 jobs. So next time you hear about a parasite running trade deficits in the billions, remember what it means in terms of American jobs.

30

Just Say No to Nintendo

*Nintendo has been accused of price-fixing and
illegally marketing its products here, putting some
American video game manufacturers—and
American workers—out of business.*

OVERVIEW

If you want to know just how dominant some Japanese manufacturers have become in the American market, consider the case of Nintendo. Unknown in the United States only ten years ago, Nintendo now controls more than 85 percent of the American video game market and generates an estimated $2.7 billion in sales from American consumers. You would think that would be enough to win some respect from the manufacturer of Game Boy and other popular video games. Wrong.

Nintendo, whose owner, Hiroshi Yamauchi, and a group of investors recently bought the Seattle Mariner baseball team, is one of the most egregious offenders of America's open trade policy.

In 1991, the Federal Trade Commission reached a settlement with Nintendo to bar it from fixing prices with its dealers and bilking Americans out of millions of dollars. According to the FTC complaint, Nintendo went so far as to set up a "snitch" network, allowing dealers to report other dealers who might be price-discounting.

The result, according to the complaint, is that Nintendo's prices never fell in six years of U.S. operations—even though similar high-tech equipment fell 50 percent in price during the same time period. The alleged illegal activity presumably cost American consumers an estimated $100 million.

Nintendo got off by rebating $25 million to consumers through discounts on a new generation of game cartridges—which ironically, sold for twice as much as the ones the company had price-fixed. Nintendo claims the settlement is not an admission of guilt.

Nintendo's alleged price-fixing tactics are only one example of how the company has extracted money from American consumers. While Nintendo has made a fortune selling its products to Americans, it produces none of its products here in this country. Its only employees are sales and marketing people, truck unloaders, and hordes of young Americans who answer telephone calls concerning how to improve play on Nintendo. While we play and pay, Nintendo is creating jobs overseas. We deserve better.

Toys "R" Us, Nintendo's biggest customer, also benefited from Nintendo's inflated prices. And the big news in 1992 from Toys "R" Us is that the company has opened retail stores in Japan. It has not been easy, confides a company official. Japanese toy manufacturers have been slow to deal directly with the American company, thereby reducing its ability to offer the deep discounts that makes the concept work so well in the United States. But paybacks can be golden. The first toy manufacturer to deal directly with Toys "R" Us in Japan? You guessed it—Nintendo.

What You Can Do

- **Despite what your kids want, you don't have to buy Nintendo.** The company doesn't deserve our business. It's as simple as that.
- **Hand-write a letter to the Chairman of Toys "R" Us.** Competitors claim that Nintendo represents 15 percent of Toys "R" Us revenues and 25 percent of its profits. The company has a vested interest in responding to consumers' complaints and opinions about Nintendo.

Write a letter stating that you do not intend to buy any more

Nintendo products after learning how anti-American the company is, and that you will tell at least three of your friends about Nintendo and about its alliance with Toys "R" Us. Mail it to:

Charles Lazarus
Chairman of the Board and Chief Operating Officer
Toys "R" Us, Inc.
461 From Road
Paramus, New Jersey 07652

• **Send away for the Atari video game catalog.** You can receive it by writing:

Atari
1196 Borregas Avenue
Sunnyvale, California 94086

Saving American Jobs While on the Job or Looking for One

31

The New Union Label

*Unions have been instrumental in improving standards of
living for U.S. workers. Now we need unions and their
members to save American jobs.*

OVERVIEW

There was a time when the battle lines in the workplace were
clearly drawn. On one side stood management, protecting
profits. On the other, unions battled tooth and nail for better
wages and greater benefits.

But times have changed. Today the battle has widened, and
management is no longer the enemy. Instead, American
workers are at war with laborers in scores of countries, all of
whom are anxious to grab the jobs that were once America's
domain and the province of its many strong unions.

So what's become of the unions? Their strength has dimin-
ished as their traditional strongholds in textiles, steel-making,
and auto manufacturing have been decimated by foreign
competition.

Is today's union member a relic of yesterday's economy? Not
necessarily. In the new world order of increased global competition, unions can play a key role in enhancing productivity and
helping America retain its place as the preeminent economic
power in the world. But whether that happens depends on how
unions and their members respond to the new realities of the
American workplace.

A Brief Case Study

Some plants go idle and lose all of their jobs, while others remain open and retain jobs. Take a look at the evolution of one Ford plant—from one of the most fractious to one of the most productive—as profiled in a *Wall Street Journal* case study to see how the union was key to keeping the plant running.

To put the story in its proper context however, it's important to understand that Ford Motor Company sold almost as many vehicles in 1978 as it did in 1988, but with half as many workers. Ford was concentrating heavily on achieving productivity gains, and by the numbers alone, seemed to be getting them.

Sure, advances in design and engineering helped a lot. But by far the most important factor in the auto makers' productivity gains involved increased cooperation with the rank and file. The workers at the Walton Hills metal stamping plant illustrate the changing and effective leadership of the United Auto Workers (UAW). Fifteen years ago, it was a different story. Back then, the Walton Hills plant idled Ford nationwide over the issue of bathroom doors.

But now, thanks in part to a partnership between labor and management, the Walton Hills workers consistently contribute to productivity gains. For example, every year since 1985, the workers have helped to reduce labor and overhead by an average of 3.2 percent. And the new team spirit has encouraged innovation on the factory floor. For example, according to the *Wall Street Journal* piece, metal press operator Bob Kubec figured a way to save sheet metal on every floor panel part he makes. Ford got $70,000 in savings every year and Bob Kubec got a $14,000 reward.

A lot of this comes down to atmosphere. Rather than standing idle, Ford workers seem to move around with a sense of purpose and intent. And the change in attitude and habits has bottom line results. According to consultant Harbour & Associates, Ford takes one-third fewer man-hours to build its cars and, as a result, enjoys a cost advantage of $795 per car over its rival, the article reports.

As sales rose in the latter '80s and older workers retired, Ford was eventually able to bring back virtually all of its former employees who wanted their former jobs. And when they hit the factory floor, they had a new appreciation for productivity and profits.

As part of its continuing efforts to foster a partnership between labor and management, Ford sponsored a number of trips to Japan so both sides could get a look at their manufacturing plants. There, John D'Amico, the local 420 president had a stunning revelation. "The Japanese didn't work harder," said D'Amico in the *Wall Street Journal*, "they simply did a better job of working together."

What You Can Do

Get involved in your union. According to union officials, it's the members who do not attend meetings or keep abreast of the issues facing the union that drag the organization back into the adversarial days of the sixties and seventies. Today, unions are more aware than ever about what it takes to survive in a competitive world. And to accomplish that goal, they are working closely with management, evaluating new production techniques and studying ways to increase productivity. Union members need to stay informed of these initiatives by being involved.

Take advantage of union training programs and opportunities. It's simple: the more you know, the more of an asset you and your union become to the company. If your union has not made a commitment to training and retraining, start asking why.

Get vocal. Unions were born because people got vocal. Use this fundamental tool to preserve the future of unions in America. If you sense your union sliding into the debilitating attitudes and practices of the past, speak up.

Pledge yourself completely. Too many members only turn to their unions when they face a strike or during contract negotiations. You—your voice and your influence—also need to be there when your union is developing new training programs, debating policy, or working with management on improving productivity.

Support labor worldwide. By doing so you help others working and living in squalor. But more important, by pressing foreign governments and industry for fairer wages and benefits, you help reduce the wage disparity between U.S. workers and their counterparts abroad. The result: American products become more competitive and jobs are generated in our own backyard.

32

Picture Yourself as a Trade Ambassador

One of America's greatest hopes for new jobs is creating demand for our products overseas. Sometimes it just takes a little chutzpah.

OVERVIEW

In earlier days, American business did not have to look any farther than its own backyard to find the sales and profits that put Americans to work. The U.S. market offered huge and easily accessible opportunities for everyone from chewing gum makers to pocket calculator manufacturers.

Today, it's a whole new ball game. As U.S. markets become more and more competitive—some to the point of saturation—American businesses are learning that the real opportunities of the 1990s and beyond lie in the emerging and awakening economies of far-off places.

But to make the leap, American businesses and the people who work for them have to start thinking locally in terms of employment and acting globally in the way they market and distribute their products and services. From Basel to Bangkok, we need to find new demand for our products that will spur production and create jobs in this country.

You don't have to be a company CEO or even an international trader to find a foreign market for your product. The world of international business is rife with stories of workaday employees who found overseas markets for a product or service and made that discovery pay off in terms of American employment.

A Brief Case Study

When orders from Canada started trickling into Trek, the Waterloo, Wisconsin-based bicycle manufacturer, no one in the company took them very seriously. Like many American companies, Trek had its hands full trying to master the U.S. market during the early 1980s. The requests got passed to Joyce Keehn, then a customer service representative for the firm.

But Keehn took the inquires plenty serious. She realized that if Canada wanted the company's bike, so too might other markets in the world—in countries that didn't share America's inventory of cars and that therefore might need pedal power to move people.

Keehn went to Trek management and begged for a chance to introduce the product overseas. "Go for it," management told her. "But don't spend any money."

Keehn slogged forward, generating correspondence, finding out about letters of credit, getting shipping rates and information, filling out Customs forms, and tackling logistical challenges.

"I got the most help from the Wisconsin Department of Commerce," notes Keehn, "but I also attended a lot of seminars where I met people and picked their brains. Most were very helpful and more than willing to share information."

By the time she was done with Canada one year later, Keehn left a distribution network of sixty-five outlets in her wake. Then, in 1989, with the blessing and confidence of Trek management, Keehn set her sights on Europe. Now Trek is in fifty-three countries, and 40 percent of the company's sales are international.

Keehn's globe-trotting produced jobs for Trek in both management and production. "Those new jobs," she says, "are the thing I'm proud of most."

What You Can Do

Become a foreign trade ambassador. No matter what your job and no matter what type of company you work for, there might be the opportunity to find a foreign market for your product.

Remember, Joyce Keehn was only a customer service representative—an order-taker—before launching Trek's international initiative. But she saw an opportunity and jumped on it. The result? A better job for Joyce—and more jobs for Americans.

Join a local international business association. You'd be surprised how many cities have organizations where American manufacturers meet to discuss overseas opportunities. Check with local colleges and universities and chambers of commerce to see what organizations are available in your area.

Don't overlook personal contacts. Have an uncle who lives in Italy? How about a cousin in Colombia? Ask them to help you research or investigate opportunities in those countries for your company's products or services. Many American businesses have cracked international markets via personal contact with employees, vendors, or friends.

Think logically. Make a list of ten countries that you think *might* need your product. Then do some research to see if that country *does* use your product. You can find that information in the *International Trade Statistics Yearbook of the United Nations*, a reference guide published by the UN and available at most major libraries. It lists product demand by countries of the world. It's often used by consultants, who get paid big bucks to find international markets for companies. You can do the same thing.

Remember, not all countries are on the same technology curve that we are in the United States. And this disparity can create foreign trade opportunities. Typewriters, for example, all but outmoded by computers here, might find an enthusiastic reception in developing countries.

Make some telephone calls. Call the embassies of the countries you think could use your product. Ask the trade representatives where you could find any information you might need, including whether the product could be imported. Ask them for any trade associations, publications, or groups that might help you in their country.

For More Information:

Subscribe to *World Trade* magazine. It's chock-full of practical advice on exporting your product. To order the magazine, write:

World Trade
500 Newport Center Drive
Newport Beach, California 92660
714-640-7070
Subscriptions cost $24 per year.

Books

Exporting From Start to Finish, L. Fargo Wells, Liberty Press, Blue Ridge Summit, Pennsylvania.

Import/Export: How to Get Started on the International Market, Carl Nelson, Blue Ridge Summit, Pennsylvania.

33

Purchasing Jobs

Leverage. You can lift the world with it. You can also use it to create and preserve American jobs.

OVERVIEW

If you invest all of your income in buying American products, you might be spending $10,000, $20,000, maybe as much as $50,000 a year to create American jobs. But what if you could spend $2 million? How many jobs do you think you could create if you spent it wisely?

Many people you know spend this much money. They are the purchasing managers at the places where you work. We need to get these people on our side. Here's why. According to a study by the National Association of Purchasing Management, the average purchasing agent in the construction and engineering industry spends $3.1 million to buy goods and services for his or her company. In the pharmaceutical industry, the average purchasing agent spends $13.3 million on supplies, equipment, and anything else the company needs. No matter what the industry, in economic terms, these people have tremendous clout, and they should use it to create and preserve American jobs.

A Brief Case Study

Diversified manufacturer Teleflex Incorporated serves aerospace, medical, automotive, marine, and industrial markets and has sales of more than $470 million. The purchasing department of the company's aerospace division has a Buy American policy in place.

133

"The reason is simple," says Bill Baker, a Teleflex purchasing manager. "We're in the aerospace business. People are up in the air when they are depending on our products. We can't have defects. With American-made components, it's much easier for us to control quality."

According to Baker, the division has a long history of buying American. Initially, it was because the company had to follow the requirements set down by the 1951 Buy American Act for government contractors. But even after the act was scuttled in the mid-seventies, Baker reports, his division kept on buying American.

Baker says that many American products appear to be more expensive, but when you start uncovering the hidden costs of European or Asian components, the playing field levels. "You need to add in shipping over the big ponds, then shipping when it gets here; you have to add in the cost of inspection and quality control overseas. And because you end up buying in very large quantities when buying overseas, you have to add in the cost of carrying the inventory. On the inspection and shipping alone, a part that starts out costing a dollar might end up really costing a dollar sixty-five."

Baker, who personally spends some $7 million on behalf of his employer, says that most of the purchasing is done with smaller companies that have less than one hundred employees. He knows that his policy and his actions put Americans to work. "Some of the shops we deal with have just four or five people, so our work is very meaningful to them. When we get busy, they get real busy and bring on more help to get the work done."

What You Can Do

Get your company to start a Buy American program. No matter what level you're at, or what you do at your company, you can help get the program going.

Write to or speak with the president, owner, general manager, or purchasing manager of your company. Say you believe the company should make it a policy to buy some or all

American-made products. Say it's a good idea, because it keeps Americans working and because it's good for the company's bottom line. Specifically:

1. You can buy American products in smaller quantities and reduce inventory costs.

2. You can exercise more control over the quality of American products.

3. American products are less expensive when you factor in the cost of quality control and transportation.

4. American-made products have a shorter lead time.

- Get a petition going among your coworkers so that you can document the support in your organization for a Buy American program.

- Draft a Buy American policy statement. The statement should describe the company's reason for adopting the program and its parameters, such as products included or excluded, or the percentage of purchases subject to the program. Send this statement to the owner or purchasing manager for his or her opinion.

- Talk directly with the purchasing manager. You might be able to jump-start a program on an informal basis. Express your feelings about the importance of purchasing American-made products.

A Final Thought

If you are involved in purchases, Teleflex's Baker urges a closer working relationship with your suppliers. "Many times our suppliers will have a hard time finding the American product we ordered. In those cases, we try to help them find sources, or sometimes we even send an engineer and a purchasing manager to their factory to show them how to make what we need so they don't have to buy it. If we are going to build manufacturing again in this country, we've got to be committed, and work together."

34

Create Your Own Job

In a tough economy, the people who get hired are those who know how to create a job when one does not exist.

OVERVIEW

"No one is hiring." That's a frequent lament of a discouraged job seeker, especially when the economy is off and job openings are rare. Truth is, however, even during economic slowdowns, businesses are still looking for top talent and good opportunities. In fact, they look harder during recessions, because they have to make every penny count. That means that if you can deliver demonstrated value or a proven ability to get results, you just might persuade an employer to make a place for you, even when he or she is not hiring.

"Ten percent of the people I place are in created positions," says Bob Gandy, a recruiter for Management Recruiters International, the world's largest head-hunting company, based in Cleveland.

"We create jobs by showing the company an individual's accomplishments. We sell their special abilities and the value they bring with them."

Gandy says he frequently knocks on the doors of businesses that are not hiring and then urges them to simply talk to a job seeker. "We market the individual's talent, and in many cases the company sees how it can benefit from those talents. Often the meeting turns into a job."

You don't need to be a nuclear physicist to create a job. You simply have to package what skills you have, and make sure that package gets delivered to someone in a position to respond to it with a job offer.

A Brief Case Study

Peter Kwak had some big-time qualifications in the financial industry. For ten years, he had worked for financial services firms, in everything from systems analysis to sales. But like thousands of others, Kwak got caught in the massive restructuring of the industry. In 1990, he was laid off.

To make himself more marketable, Kwak invested one month of his own time and money developing a data-base software program unlike anything else on the market.

"I developed the program so that I could speak intelligently to companies that needed someone who knew data-base systems," says Kwak. "I also developed it because if someone could take advantage of the program they might hire me along with it."

Sure enough, someone did see a lot of value in what Kwak was doing. It was the American Red Cross—which liked the program, hired Kwak, and moved him from Seattle, where he had created the program, to New York City.

"They didn't have a position for me" says Kwak. "I created the job by using my programming skills. My own initiative impressed them so much that they hired me."

What You Can Do

Create a job for yourself. You have to have an imagination, some creativity, and a willingness to take a risk and maybe even work without wages for a period, but it pays off. And if you don't have a job, what do you have to lose by trying? Here's what to do:

1. Identify your top ten skills and then determine what industries and businesses are most in need of them.
2. Write a detailed, but brief, plan of how your skills could improve a company's product line, sales figures, morale, expansion plans, etc.
3. Submit your plan, along with a resume, to the targeted firm.
4. Arrange a meeting with the person you've written to. There, emphasize the value you bring to the table and how your skills and your plan can help the firm meet its objectives.

For the record, here are ten creative ways that you can make a job for yourself.

- If you're in real estate development and management, create a survey and send it to twenty-five commercial tenants to determine their satisfaction with their current management company. Find two or three dissatisfied tenants, then send the details of your survey to prospective employers with an explanation of how you would convert these tenants into clients.

- If you're a teacher looking for a job, offer to teach drama, coach a sports team, work with the band, or perform other volunteer service to become known within a school district and be seen as indispensable.

- If you are an architect, offer to do a project on speculation as a way to show your abilities.

- If you are in public relations, challenge an agency to let you arrange media coverage for an event or a client. Then get the press!

- If you are a controller, offer to review a firm's operating costs, then suggest ten ways it can save money.

- If you are a cook, create a signature entree or dessert for the restaurant you want to work for, and submit the recipe for it or the dish along with your credentials.

- If your skills lie in advertising, review magazines and newspapers and identify ads you believe do not work. Revamp the ads and send your ideas, along with your resume and qualifications, to the company. Will you upset company management? Maybe. But if it likes your ideas, someone might give you a call.

- If you're a restaurant manager, study closely the restaurant you would like to work for and then develop a marketing and promotion plan to increase sales 15 percent. Arrange a meeting where you can explain the plan.

- If you are a salesperson, develop a list of fifty qualified leads and then persuade the sales manager to meet with you to review the list.

• If you train people to use computers, offer to interview company personnel and determine their need for training. Then submit a proposal for the training, along with an analysis of how much money the firm would save by hiring you as its trainer.

Good luck!

35

Get Passionate About Your Work

Productivity is the key to retaining and creating jobs.
Want to give America's productivity a boost?
Embrace your occupation with enthusiasm.

OVERVIEW

During the second World War, the federal government printed morale-boosting posters for display in various public buildings. One of the most famous showed a woman in full welding gear, with this headline: "America's Answer: Production!" In large measure, we won the war because we outproduced our enemies. In today's economic war, the same idea still holds true. We can win with productivity. You see, productivity is the key to American competitiveness and the creation of American jobs. When we produce more products and services faster and more efficiently, we make it harder, much harder, on foreign manufacturers trying to create jobs outside of this country.

How can we become more productive? By becoming passionate about our life's work. People who are happy are more productive, period. And it's an idea that is, well, passionately embraced by employment professionals.

Rhoda Cohen, an employment counselor at the Jewish Employment and Vocational Center, says, "I absolutely believe that people who love their jobs are more productive workers, as well as being happier individuals overall." Rhoda's right. Too often, Americans settle for jobs they are not passionate about. As a result, they come in late, they leave early, and they work at half the pace they would if they were happy.

Sure the economy absorbs these inefficiencies, but cumulatively, it hurts. Some repetitive jobs are hard to get passionate about, that's true. But in our automated workplace, even that is changing. Twenty-five years ago, our autoworkers performed the same mind-numbing task hour after hour. Today, they're being asked for their input, about everything from factory design to sales and marketing. Productivity is the key to saving American jobs. And passion is the key to productivity. Read on for an inspiring illustration of how the two go hand in hand and create jobs for Americans.

A Brief Case History

"I wanted to illustrate children's books since the sixth grade," says Kevin O'Malley, a children's book illustrator in Baltimore. "The moment I saw the book *Where the Wild Things Are*, I was hooked—I knew illustration was my passion."

Immediately after graduation from art school, Kevin went in search of his first assignment. The competition was intense. "About five thousand children's books are published each year," says Kevin. "That might sound encouraging, but by my estimates, there's something like fifty-thousand manuscripts submitted to publishers each year as well." When Kevin asked a fellow illustrator how much room he'd had when he'd negotiated his first contract, the answer was ominous. "None," his friend said.

It was ten years before Kevin landed his first assignment. "I had jobs as a dishwasher, a bartender, and a Christmas display designer while I tried to get published," says Kevin. "I just kept plugging away, submitting work that I had done during my lunch hour, evenings, whenever." Over the course of a decade, Kevin says, he received more than 300 rejection letters. "Sure they hurt," he says, "but they also feel good, because each 'no' meant I was one step closer to a 'yes,' and because I was doing what I really loved."

Passion pays off. In the winter of 1990, publisher Stewart,

Tabori & Chang took a chance on one of Kevin's books, *Froggy Went A-Courtin'*. It was his big break. "Once you are published, people look at you differently," says Kevin. All totaled, Kevin now has ten illustrated books under his belt, with four books currently in print. "I could never produce that kind of volume unless I was happy with what I was doing," he says. "I saw my father work himself into a heart problem over a job he didn't like. I decided that would never be me. My job is not easy—the hours, the competition, the deadlines—but I can do it well, because I love what I'm doing."

Kevin's passion is also giving the economy a big shot in the arm. The 25,000 copies of his books in print are selling for an average price of $11.95. That's some $298,000 flowing back to printers, publishers, and bookstores, which they are putting to work in the form of new projects and new jobs. Kevin's young, just thirty-one years old. How many dollars and jobs do you think he will pump into our economy over the next thirty years simply because he is passionate about his occupation?

What You Can Do

Join the battle. Help America win. We may not be on the verge of a world war, but in terms of economic wars, we've got the fight of our lives on our hands. Get passionate about your job. Here are some simple, and some not so simple, ways to do this.

Ask for additional responsibilities. Many people find that while they like their company, they do not like their specific duties. Spend some time considering tasks or duties that you would attack with a passion. Then ask your boss or supervisor if you can do them, if only on a trial basis and for an hour a day. You'll find these new responsibilities will also change your attitude about your existing duties.

Ask for a new position within your company. Explain to your immediate supervisor that you like the company, but that you need a set of responsibilities more in line with your skills and personality. Your employer probably recognizes the high cost of rehiring and the value of an experienced employee, and may be more receptive than you think.

Find a new employer. You may like what you do, but find you are at odds with your employer. Gather a list of companies in your industry that are located nearby and write the president a letter. Tell him or her you enjoy working in the industry, but that you need to find an employer who appreciates your enthusiasm. Ask if he or she has any advice for finding such an employer.

Change occupations. According to the Bureau of Labor Statistics, about 10 percent of the labor force changes occupations each year. For many this is the only road to fulfillment and productivity. There's a theory, and a book by the same name, that goes like this: *Do What You Love, the Money Will Follow* (Dell). It's by organizational psychologist Marsha Sinetar. In it, she says, "Choosing our work allows us to enter into that work willingly, enthusiastically, and mindfully."

Join the ranks of the self-employed. Though not for the faint of heart, you will find yourself in good company. Link Resources, a New York City market research and consulting firm, reports that 12.1 million people are self-employed and work out of their homes, and that the number is growing. And, the company says, in 1991 these people, combined with employees who work for a company out of their homes, spent more than $25 billion on home office equipment and telecommunications services.

Turn your hobby into a part-time occupation. It may not be practical to jump into the ranks of the self-employed wholesale, but you can test the waters. That's what nights and weekends are for! And remember, when someone buys your product, that's more money that you will spend at someone else's business.

36

The Non-Layoff

If we all bear the burden of the difficult times, we can all be present to share in the good times as well.

OVERVIEW

The Department of Labor conservatively estimates that some 5.6 million Americans have been displaced from their jobs over the past five years. Sometimes with numbers so large we lose our perspective. But for every person in that statistic, as well as their families and dependents, the loss of work is traumatic. Not only that, but the loss of these jobs has a domino effect that hurts American competitiveness and productivity. Then there's the social cost of lost homes, savings, and self-esteem. Health and marital problems, and even suicide, are just a few of the more visible side effects of wholesale layoffs.

The real tragedy? Sometimes layoffs really aren't necessary. When workers stick together and management keeps an open mind, layoffs can often be avoided. The key is spreading the shortage of work among all the workers, not just a select few. It's called the **non-layoff**, or the **job rotation**. Whatever its name, it's saving American jobs and paying big dividends for the companies and employees that have put the concept into action.

A Brief Case History

Like most builders, Bread Loaf Construction Co., in Middlebury, Vermont, rode the ups and downs of the construction industry. But unlike many construction companies, Bread Loaf put a plan in place to keep all 150 of its workers on the payroll. The idea was put into action when general economic conditions conspired with the cyclical nature of construction. Rather than handing out pink slips, the company asked the crew on one of its major projects to work two out of every three weeks until further notice.

"The immediate reduction in costs helped us stay competitive," says Peter Mitchell, Bread Loaf's director of business development. "And of course, the advantage to our employees was that they all remained employed and were able to keep their benefits current."

Another advantage for Bread Loaf, according to Mitchell, was that the company could bid on projects, knowing that it had the skilled, high-quality work force in place to do the job right and on time. And sure enough, within a few months Bread Loaf did win more business—and brought everyone back full-time.

Mitchell feels that employees appreciated the company's efforts to keep the "family" together, and that it showed in their work. "Morale is a key factor in the construction business," says Mitchell. "If our laborers out in the field feel secure in their jobs, they are more likely to pay attention to details. It may sound corny, but it's true that happy workers work smarter, faster, and they do it right the first time. You can't imagine the added cost of construction if we had to constantly do things over again because of human error."

Word of Bread Loaf's program spread in the construction circles of Vermont. "We got a lot of calls from other firms that wanted to know how we did it. I think they were interested because they wanted to retain good employees in tough times. We were happy to share our experiences with them. After all, one of the big lessons we learned is that when things get difficult, you have to pull together."

What You Can Do

Pull together for American jobs. If you are an employee, try to gain a consensus among your fellow employees and secure their commitment to participate in a rotational layoff. When you have done this, write a detailed letter to the president of the company, and send a copy to the person in charge of human resources. You want to get them talking. Ask to schedule a meeting with the president and anyone else he or she believes should be present. When you get there, keep an open mind, recognize the concerns of the company owner or president, and be ready to offer some compromises. But also make sure that the top brass understands how job rotation can prevent layoffs from occurring:

1. When employees go, business goes with them, plain and simple.
2. Layoffs are a self-fulfilling numbers game. Cut staff by 10 percent, and watch sales follow the same trend.
3. There's a huge cost a business must bear down the road to retrain new workers.
4. Layoffs decimate morale, and as a result hamper productivity.

If you are an employer, start considering how this plan would work at your company. Formulate the logistics of rotational layoffs in each of your key departments or functional areas, then write a plan for how it would work in practice so that if and when the time comes, your employees have a blueprint. Develop a strategy for introducing and promoting the plan among employees if its application becomes necessary. Discuss the plan with your senior managers. Gain their support. Most important, solicit their feedback on areas that will pose special challenges, and ask them to formulate ideas about how to overcome these problems.

Other Angles

In corporate boardrooms, mergers and acquisitions seem to make sense and the word "synergy" comes up often. But in the workplace, mergers and acquisitions often create redundant jobs and can result in massive layoffs. In banking, where deregulation has led to lots of merger and acquisition activity, the problem has become rampant. Some banks, however, have developed unique programs to save the jobs that often get lost after the dust has settled. Gus Tolson, corporate employment manager at CoreStates Banks, talks about one of his favorite programs. "About six months before a planned acquisition, we go into the organization we are acquiring and hold a jobs fair, posting the listings that we have at that point in time. We allow employees to apply for the jobs, and, if accepted, the organization we are acquiring cooperates by letting that person go, and filling their position with temporary workers."

Tolson says this "lend-lease program," as he calls it, requires advance planning and a good dose of cooperation between the companies party to the transaction. But he says the payoff is large. "The employees have more options than if they simply wait for something to happen, and when jobs are accepted, it gives the employees a chance to gradually acclimate themselves to the new corporate culture."

Do you see a merger or acquisition in your company's future? Write a letter to the president of your company and suggest a jobs fair prior to its consummation. A key selling point? Easing the transition for employees will enhance the likelihood of the company's success after the deal is done. Now that's synergy!

SECTION 6

Becoming an Activist
for American Jobs

37

Foreign Product Amnesty Day

*You can sponsor a media event to drive home
the importance of saving American jobs.*

OVERVIEW

Advocacy groups—groups that lobby and agitate for change—draw attention to issues through well-publicized promotions that draw free media.

The struggle to save American jobs requires a concerted publicity effort. Maintaining America's standard of living by giving our family, friends, and neighbors the right to work is of primary concern to everyone, yet few know how much they can do about it. Heightening that awareness is what Foreign Product Amnesty Days are all about.

What You Can Do

- **A Foreign Product Amnesty Day.** The goal of this day is to increase public awareness of the need to buy American to keep jobs in this country. It's intended to provide a high-profile event to attract the media, educate consumers, and help charities.

- It's simple. A local community group, either a civic or business association, sponsors a one-day event where consumers can turn in foreign-made products, which are then donated to a charity or to needy families in the area. In return, consumers promise to buy a new, like-kind American-made product.

151

How to Do It

- Start by enlisting the help of a local Rotary or other community service group, chamber of commerce, church, or American Legion or other veterans' association. Decide on a charity and enlist its help to publicize and organize the event.

- Conduct the event on a Saturday, on-site at either the charity's headquarters or at a church, a school, or the offices of the sponsoring association.

- Publicize it well through the newsletter of the sponsoring association and through other promotional ideas—putting signs up on bulletin boards in churches, supermarkets, and community centers; going to local senior centers, schools, and other community gathering places and telling administrators and leaders about the program; and designing fliers and delivering them to the doors of consumers.

- Include local retailers in the event. After all, consumers will be looking for American-made products to replace the ones they donate. Local hardware and variety stores, small-appliance retailers, and electronics businesses are certain to see sales increase as a result of the event. Ask them to chip in a few dollars to help sponsor an advertisement in the local newspaper. Also, ask them to identify American-made products in their stores so consumers will know which products to purchase.

- Crank up the publicity machine. Contact your local media—radio, television, daily and weekly newspapers. At radio and television stations, you will want to get information to either a news director, assignment editor, or producer. At newspapers, your best bet is the business editor or general-assignment editor.

Any news releases you produce should be submitted at least a week before your event. Here's a sample news release:

FROM:
(Your Group's Name)
(Your Group's Address)

(A Contact Name)
(A Contact Telephone Number)
(Date)

For Immediate Release:

Rotary Sponsors Foreign Product Amnesty Day

In an attempt to save American jobs by encouraging local consumers to buy American-made products, the (town's name) Rotary Club is sponsoring a Foreign Product Amnesty Day, Saturday, (date, time, and place).

The event offers consumers the chance to hand in foreign-made products, which will be donated to needy families through (name of charity).

In return, consumers promise to replace the donated product with similar, American-made products. To help consumers find American-made products, Rotary officials will be handing out the names and addresses of local retailers who have agreed to feature American-made products in support of the event. In addition, the Rotary has developed its own list of American-certified products.

"With so many of our townspeople losing their jobs due to foreign competition, we thought now was the time to do something about it," says Rotary president (name). "We hope the event will increase public awareness to how we're damaging ourselves by not buying products made by Americans."

The idea for the event comes from the book *50 Things You Can Do to Save American Jobs*, published by Carol Publishing Group.

"We think it's great that the people of (town's name) are following our advice and working on the local level to make a difference in this country," says Greg Matusky, the book's coauthor. "If more Americans do the same, we can save jobs and put our families, friends, and neighbors back to work."

For more information about the event, call (telephone number).

One Final Note

After sending your news releases, make sure to personally call the media and invite them to attend the event.

Sources

Consult with local retailers to determine which products are American-made and whether they are locally available. You also might want to read:

> *The Patriotic Consumer, How to Buy American*
> Edited by Anne Grant and Web Burrell
> Andrews and McMeel, A Universal Press Syndicate Company
> 4900 Main Street
> Kansas City, Missouri 64112

and

> *Made in the USA*
> Made in the USA Foundation
> 35 Wisconsin Circle, Suite 200
> Chevy Chase, Maryland 20815
> 301-718-2671

38

The Enemy Is Us

*Who is forming public policy on trade
and other issues that affect American jobs?
More and more, it's think tanks and lobbyists
funded by foreigners.*

OVERVIEW

In America, consensus should be driven by a free market of ideas and opinions. But too often that free market is being monopolized by Americans who for a price will lobby for causes beneficial to foreign companies but devastating to American workers.

Pat Choate, author of *Agents of Influence*, estimates that the Japanese alone spend $500 million a year to influence American hearts and souls by buying lobbyists and other opinion makers in this country.

These "Guccis"—$350-an-hour former legislators or government officials—understand how policy is made in this country and use their inside knowledge to undermine initiatives that could spur job creation here.

It's a big business, one that includes former Cabinet members, trade representatives, and White House aides. It also involves some of the most revered think tanks in this country.

Think tanks are bastions of intellectual thought, places where policy is studied for the consumption of government, the press, and the general public. Many think tanks bill themselves as unconnected and unbiased. Yet some of this country's mainstream think tanks are in part funded, either directly or indirectly, by foreign money, through grants and other means.

155

Not surprisingly, these think tanks espouse foreign policies disguised as what they think the American people want to hear. Think tankers often comment on any number of trade issues and even testify before Congress, thereby getting their fair share of press. When they make news, there's no indication that these "thinkers" are paid by private interests.

Some of the Worst Offenders

According to researchers who work with Pat Choate, some of the best-known and most often-sourced think tanks are involved in the foreign money grab game. They include:

- The Institute for International Economics in Washington, D.C. During the 1980s, the Institute argued that Japanese trade barriers played a minor role in the U.S. trade deficit. The barriers haven't fallen and our trade deficit is still climbing. Where does some of the Institute's money come from? *Answer*: the Germans and the Japanese.

- The American Enterprise Institute in Washington, D.C. Another conservative/neoconservative think tank, it believes that bilateral trade deficits (Japan selling us lots of products and not buying many of ours) are no problem. Tell that to American workers without jobs. Again, it's Japanese money that in part funds these researchers.

- The Center for Strategic and International Studies in Washington, D.C. The Center has come under fire for accepting money from Toyota to fund a chair for Japanese studies and then consulting with the company about who is appointed.

What You Can Do

According to Alan Tonelson of the Economic Strategy Institute, think tanks are important sources for the press, which uses their research papers and cites them as objective sources of information. To prevent that from happening:

- Write letters to reporters at magazines and newspapers who report on foreign trade and foreign affairs. Alert them to the problem of influence in American think tanks. Urge reporters to ask their sources whether they or the organizations they represent receive foreign money. Tell them to report these biases when citing such sources.

• Call radio and television talk shows that frequently discuss politics or the economy. Ask those who argue the case for unbridled free trade whether they or the organizations they represent receive foreign monies in the form of contributions, grants, loans, or stipends. You just might make some of them squirm.

• Join United We Stand, Ross Perot's grass-roots government watchdog group. Perot brought the issue of foreign influence to light during his bid for the presidency in 1992. He's made the issue an important plank in his organization's ongoing platform. To join, call 800-925-4000. Membership is $15.

And Don't Forget

Read *Agents of Influence* (Simon & Schuster, New York, New York). It provides keen insight into how foreign governments are undermining American public policy for their own benefit.

39

Advertise for American Jobs

*Here's how you can win free advertising for
those looking for jobs in your town.*

OVERVIEW

They used to advertise fallout shelters so that when the
shrapnel started flying, you knew where to go. It's the same
with jobs. Almost every city or town in America stands a
chance of taking a hit, of waking up one morning and finding
that suddenly the town's biggest employer is closing its doors—
and along with it, 100, 1,000, maybe 10,000 jobs.

If that should happen, there's one plan of action you can take
immediately to help others and yourself find employment. It
can start at your local newspaper.

A Brief Case Study

During March of 1992, New England was wracked with
unemployment, the region's entire economy devastated by
recession. Unemployment rates were running in double digits
and the *Boston Globe*, with a circulation of 505,000, decided to do
something about it. The newspaper offered free classified ads to
anyone in need of a job. Unemployed people could run between
three and five lines about themselves, worth about $50, for free.

The response was overwhelming, according to the *Globe's*
Rick Gulla. "We received ten thousand ads in the first ten days,"
he reports. The paper began running two solid pages of the free
classifieds daily, and didn't stop for two weeks. Every ad
appeared once, until the *Globe* had run all ads.

158

To enhance the effectiveness of the program, the *Boston Globe* sent letters to the top one hundred public companies in the state, telling them about the ads and urging the companies to use them as a resource. They also posted advisories with area chambers of commerce. And finally, all twenty pages of the ads were reprinted and made available by mail to any company that requested a copy.

According to Gulla, the *Boston Globe* invested about $60,000 in promoting the idea and producing the ads. Sounds like a lot. And it is. But the *Globe* got back its investment more than tenfold through free publicity and good community relations. "The publicity was tremendous," says Gulla. "CNN, *USA Today*, the 'Today' show all carried the story. Judging from the calls and letters, we know people got jobs. And we even got letters from people who just wanted to say thanks for trying to help out. It felt real good."

What You Can Do

When a layoff or wholesale cutback afflicts your town, approach your newspaper about doing a free classified ad section for job seekers. You have to be an ambassador and a diplomat. But most of all you have to take the lead.

Call or write the publisher of your newspaper and arrange a meeting. Tell them about the idea and make sure to tell them about the efforts of the *Boston Globe*. Ask them what resources they need to get the program going. They might need volunteers to staff the phones and take down ads, public-service announcements on local radio and television promoting the program, or help in getting the chamber of commerce behind the program.

Here are three key points to make in your pitch:

1. It's in the newspaper's self-interest to get the town back on its feet. After all, the newspaper is supported by local businesses that depend on townspeople as customers. If unemployment remains high, you better believe ad sales will eventually be hurt.

2. The paper will earn significant goodwill from its readers and advertisers.

3. The paper will likely earn substantial publicity for its efforts.

Inside Tip

CNBC, the cable network, has announced plans to launch the Career Television Network (CTN) this year for forty-five million subscribers nationwide. Companies seeking employees will post the openings with the network, which will report on them, much as CNN reports on the news. People who are looking for jobs can call and relay information about their skills and experience, which will then be formatted onto an electronic resume that can run up to fourteen pages. A processing fee of $4 will be charged to the job seeker. The companies will pick up the fee to advertise the openings and will have access to the resumes that CTN collects.

40

Volunteer to Save a Job

One sure way to create or preserve American jobs is to pass along our skills and experience to those who need it.

OVERVIEW

When times get tough, Americans pull together and help one another. One of the ways we do this is through volunteering. Unlike any other nation, America has a tradition of volunteering. In fact, we are almost fanatical about it. Take a look at these figures supplied by the Points of Light Foundation:

- 94.2 million people volunteered 20.5 *billion* hours, valued at $176 billion, in 1991.

- 51 percent of Americans volunteered, and the average commitment was more than four hours a week.

- The business sector accounts for the fastest-growing pool of volunteer resources, and increased its number of volunteer programs 50 percent between 1985 and 1990.

Now it's time to take this spirit of dedication and community service and direct it toward one of the most pressing issues facing us: jobs.

Almost every one of us is blessed with some special skill or knowledge. Some of us know how to read. Some of us know math. Others can build a business, sell, negotiate, operate a computer, a press punch, or a forklift. Whatever skills you have acquired, someone else in your community can surely use them to land a job or create one.

161

What You Can Do

Volunteer. Here are four ways to do it with a focus on creating jobs for Americans.

1. Literacy programs. When someone gains the ability to read a help wanted ad or sign, his or her chances of getting a job increase immeasurably. Also, many literacy programs teach study skills so that workers can qualify for or get the most out of work-related or work-sponsored training.

If you know a second language, you are especially valuable. Many literacy programs actually aid the business community by running English as a Second Language programs. In one instance, the jobs of Spanish-speaking workers were placed in jeopardy when the clothing factory that employed them upgraded its machinery. No one could teach these workers how to use the equipment. But by enrolling them in a second-language course on the premises, the workers were able to absorb enough English, and the necessary training, to preserve their jobs.

If you are interested in literacy, call your local library. It has information about local programs that you can assist. You can also check the phone book for literacy, in either the white pages or under Human Services in the blue pages. If that doesn't work, call the Literacy Hotline at 800-228-8813. It's a national line that can give you a lead on programs near where you live.

2. Executive Skills. Are you a retired executive? Call SCORE, which stands for Service Corps of Retired Executives. This program, sponsored by the Small Business Administration, will line you up with small businesses that need help in accounting, financing, manufacturing, product development, marketing, computers, human resources, or whatever. If you possess executive skills, SCORE will put them to work for a small business.

There's also ACE, or Active Corps of Executives, another SBA program, this one for executives who have a job but still have some time on their hands. For both programs, contact the Small Business Administration. Write U.S. SBA, 409 Third Street SW,

Washington, D.C. 20416. Or call 202-205-6600 to get the telephone number of your regional SBA office.

3. Youth Guidance. Junior Achievement helps prepare kids for the world of work through innovative school-affiliated programs. Call or write:

Junior Achievement
One Education Way
Colorado Springs, Colorado 80906
719-540-8000.

4. Mentoring. Mentors are people who volunteer to offer ongoing guidance and counsel to someone following in a career path similar to their own. "Mentoring is the third most powerful relationship in someone's life, next to family and love relationships," according to Richard Tye, director of the Uncommon Individual Foundation. There is no national mentoring program or center, but call your local chamber of commerce. If it doesn't sponsor a mentoring program, it should know an organization nearby that does. If that fails, call the Uncommon Individual Foundation at 215-964-1642. It can point you in the right direction.

Not sure if any of these organizations are up your alley? Call United Way Action Centers. They have local offices around the country that can help you find out about the range of volunteer opportunities and needs near you. Look in the blue pages of your telephone book under Human Services. If that fails, call the United Way in Alexandria, Virginia at 703-836-7100.

Another source to help you determine where you might volunteer most effectively is the Points of Light Foundation. Write:

Manager of Information Services
Points of Light Foundation
736 Jackson Place
Washington, D.C. 20503

The organization prefers requests in writing, but if you must call, the number is 202-408-5162.

A Final Thought

Looking for a job? Many people actually get jobs through volunteering. Once an organization recognizes the value of your skills or sees the need to expand a service beyond the scope of what can reasonably be expected from a volunteer, it can turn into a regular job.

41

You *Can* Fight City Hall

*How Americans can make sure their city
and state governments buy American.*

OVERVIEW

Cities, states, townships, and municipalities spend an estimated $38 billion a year to buy everything from computers and police cruisers to park benches and subway cars. It's big business, and one tailor-made for American-made products and services. After all, it's our tax money they're spending. Shouldn't we have the right to perform the work necessary to supply these products?

The City of Los Angeles didn't think so. Last year, the Los Angeles County Transportation Commission signed a $121.8 million contract with Japanese-owned Sumitomo Corporation of America to build driverless train cars for the City's Metro Green Line. But the deal didn't go through. Californians, already smarting from layoffs in the electronics and computer industries, did something about it. They joined forces—unions, industry, politicians, and the general public—and raised cain. In a noisy outcry of public outrage, they made the county delay the project and change the way it procures products, in order to give American companies preferential consideration when awarding big-ticket public contracts.

What You Don't Know

Most states, cities, and municipalities rely on procurement procedures outlined in city charters or state regulations when they make major purchases. The process typically requires the state or city to advertise for sealed bids from recognized suppliers and contractors. While the federal government has provisions granting preferential treatment to American-made products, towns, states, and cities are not required to give American workers any such break.

In fact, when the time comes to buy products, many local bureaucrats argue against Americans. "Our responsibility is to make sure we spend taxpayer money wisely," says a buyer with the City of Philadelphia. "If that means going overseas, that's what we will do." But then again, this buyer's work is safe. She works for America's biggest employer—the government. What's it to her if 250 Americans lose their jobs when a Japanese company gets an order for electrical cable, or subway, cars, or anything else?

What You Can Do

- **Send a wake-up call to the bureaucrats.** It's about time we send a wake-up call to callous bureaucrats. If Americans aren't making things, *no one* will be paying taxes. No matter how insulated some people think they are from the desperate situation working Americans face, we're all in this together.

- **Learn how your town government works. Does it have a preferential clause for American-made products and services?** If not, lobby local government for change. As Kenneth Desowitz, a certified purchasing manager and senior buyer for Los Angeles, says, "The voters demanded that we become more sensitive to the plight of American workers, and we did."

- **Learn the schedule of your town meetings.** Most towns are required to hold public meetings at which procurement specifications are discussed and voted on before being advertised. Working with town officials, you might be able to craft specifications that give the advantage to American firms.

- **Write letters.** They work! Write to your township or borough managers. Tell them how the City of Los Angeles changed its procurement rules to help American workers. Explain that now more than ever we need to carefully invest taxpayers' money. More and more, that means investing in getting Americans back to work!

THE LOS ANGELES SOLUTION

Los Angelenos applied so much pressure that they forced their city government to hold a referendum on changing procurement practices. The result? Residents voted to change the city charter and enact a "preferential clause" in the buying process. Under the clause, local companies that submit a higher bid than foreign companies are given the opportunity to adjust it so that it falls within 10 percent of the foreign bid, at which point their bid will be accepted.

In the case of the subway cars, the jury is still out as to whether an American firm will win the contract. There simply aren't that many American firms left in the business. But at least Los Angelenos made a statement that is sure to secure future U.S. jobs when the time comes to make similar purchases.

Sources

Check your local library and town hall for the rules and regulations your community must follow. Your state government can also help you understand how your town purchases services or products.

42

Win a Business for Your Town

*How some residents lured a Japanese manufacturer
to their small town and created 450 jobs.*

OVERVIEW

It is a familiar story. Morresville, North Carolina, had been a prosperous Southern town thanks to hardworking people who toiled in the area's textile mills. But when the textile industry headed farther south, Morresville's 10,000 residents lost their biggest source of jobs. The town could have been left for dead. But the people were too proud and too resourceful. Instead of drifting to other locations, they hung together, worked together, and eventually persuaded a major Japanese manufacturer to set up shop and hire 450 townspeople.

Luring businesses to a particular location is one of our country's newest methods of economic development. Years ago, there was little a town, county, or state—or you as an individual—could do to entice a manufacturer to relocate. Today, it's a whole different ball game, with professional marketers selling companies around the world on the benefits of various cities in the United States.

There are trade-offs. Foreign and domestic firms often expect and receive generous concessions on taxes, training, and out-and-out financial support before accepting an invitation to open shop. But towns like Morresville are ready to deal with that in return for a piece of the global job market.

HOW MORRESVILLE DID IT

"We didn't use the Madison Avenue approach," says Homer Faulk, economic developer for Morresville's chamber of commerce. Instead, according to Faulk, the people of Morresville relied on teamwork to persuade Matsushita to locate there.

At full production, in one plant alone, Matsushita Compressor Corporation of America will produce one out of every three compressors used in air conditioners here. The company learned about Morresville by accident when it was scouting U.S. locations for a $120 million plant. North Carolina holds many advantages for foreign firms, including a Right to Know law that, among other things, allows nonunion workers to continue to work during strikes.

But Morresville offered some additional benefits. In order to attract new businesses, the townspeople had founded a nonprofit group, the South Iredell Community Development Corporation, to develop 500 acres for commercial use. The land already had sewer and gas hookups. The town agreed not to annex the property for five years, which allowed Matsushita to avoid taxes for that term.

"We made concessions, but it's rare that a town of ten thousand can be in the running for attracting a giant of industry," says Faulk. In the end, Faulk and the people of Morresville believe it wasn't the tax break that did the convincing. Rather, it was the unique private-public partnership they were able to put in place.

From the first meeting, Morresville was serious about showing its commitment to its Japanese suitors. The mayor, school superintendent, chairman of the county commission, and a hospital administrator showed up to introduce the town's government, schools, and health care system. Townspeople took the Japanese to lunch on a local paddleboat and to dinner in Charlotte. The schools offered to train teachers in Japanese language and culture.

Matsushita credits the town spirit with winning its business. "Businesses can find property everywhere, and they can often win tax credits," says Tina Robertson, personnel and community relations manager for Matsushita. "It was the intense feeling of trust that Morresville was able to create that ultimately tipped the scale in their favor."

Since starting production in March 1991, the plant has produced a million compressors and employment has stayed steady at more than 400.

What You Can Do

- **Make a play for your town.** Start with your town fathers. Find out who, if anybody, is responsible for economic development. Make sure he or she is in contact with state and county economic development councils.

  If no one is responsible, contact the state or county economic development council. Their telephone numbers are usually located in the blue pages of the telephone book. Most economic development councils employ people whose sole job is to identify and target companies that might have an interest in locating in their state or county. Ask for a list of companies that have requested site studies or information from the council during the past three years. See if their criteria match your town assets. If so, promote that fact to your state or county economic development council. If that fails, go directly to the company. Find out who makes site location decisions. Get on the telephone and start talking.

- **Make your town more attractive to industry.** The people of Morresville worked to improve the infrastructure of their town to make it more attractive to business. You can do the same by urging your town to upgrade sewage and water facilities and improve road and rail access. You should also work to develop relationships between educators, business people, town officials, and hospital administrators. Ask professionals in town to identify five strengths the community has to offer. Develop this into a fact sheet that explains the advantages of doing business in your town.

- **Involve the townspeople in your mission.** Labor is often the single most critical factor businesses look at when choosing a location. Encourage your neighbors to actively express their desire to have the business locate there.

  When Klochner-Pentaplast, a German manufacturer of plastic packaging, was deciding to locate a plant in Virginia, the deal was clinched when a local farmer stood up during a town meeting and made a tearful plea to Klochner executives to give the town's young people a reason to stay near family. "Literally, we could have gone anywhere," says Harry Van Beek, the company's American-based president. "But a big consideration was who wanted us."

- **Pressure your state economic development council to promote your town or county to those businesses seeking relocation?** How? Send a letter to your state secretary of economic development or secretary of commerce. Here's a format you might want to follow:

Dear Secretary Johnson,

We're hearing a lot about the tremendous job your office is doing to recruit new business to the state. The people of this state deserve the jobs and opportunity you're creating.

Now I am asking your office to place special emphasis on promoting (name of town and county).

As you know, this area of the state offers excellent access to two major highways—I-45 and the Northwest Beltway. In addition, we have many industrial sites in place including a new industrial park that's perfect for light manufacturers as well as warehousing and supply businesses.

Can you please alert your development staff to these and other business advantages of our area and ask them to help us create jobs and opportunity for our children?

Thank you for your interest.

Sincerely,

Will a letter work? One letter may do little. But five or six speak volumes. Secretaries of economic development are politically appointed. They have a vested interest in listening to their constituents. A cry for help from a town or county is likely to be heard, if it's loud enough.

Sources

Plants, Sites & Parks
10100 West Sample Road,
  Suite 201
Coral Springs, Florida
  33065
305-753-2660

Area Development
400 Post Avenue
Westbury, New York 11590
516-338-0900

Expansion Management
1301 Spruce Street
Boulder, Colorado 80302
303-939-8440

Business Facilities
P.O. Box 2060
Red Bank, New York 07701
908-842-7433
(This publication also has
a "Site Seekers Guide" in
its January issue, which
lists economic development
councils nationwide.)

43

Banking on American Jobs

Banks can no longer sit on the sidelines. We need them to step up to the plate and start lending again, because their loans mean jobs.

OVERVIEW

We've lost jobs in this country because many banks have stopped lending money. In some ways, it's easy to understand why. If they pay you 3 percent for your deposits, and earn 6 or 7 percent on risk-free government securities, why lend? And unfortunately, this is the trend. According to the Federal Reserve Bank, as of June 1992, banks had $598.5 billion in business loans on their books versus holdings of government securities totaling $607.3 billion. What could be worse? By doing this, banks are actually helping the government finance deficit spending. They are in effect siphoning capital into the useless economic backwaters of pork-barrel spending.

But this is macroeconomics. In small-town America, it hurts. Take Grand Rapids, Michigan. All totalled, residents and businesses have some $508 million in bank deposits. But the banks there made only about $5 million in local loans. What does it mean? Grand Rapids' capital is literally being sucked away, taking with it the area's potential for economic development and new jobs.

Let's face it, creating or preserving American jobs takes money. When loans are made for housing developments, for new businesses, for business expansion, people get hired and jobs are created. When banks don't lend, when they sit idle and collect interest, Americans sit idle too.

173

And that's why we need our banks and other lenders to step up to the plate and lend money. We need them to recycle deposits into the kinds of loans that put people to work. In many cases, they don't need to lend much. They just need to take some risk, and lend.

A Brief Case Study

When Tom and Cindy Le visited Seattle on vacation in the late eighties, they fell in love with the city and decided to settle there. Picking up stakes and moving was no big deal for them. After all, both had immigrated from Vietnam in the mid-seventies.

An industrious couple, they found jobs at a convenience store, where Tom worked as manager and Cindy kept track of inventory. Although the wages were adequate, the couple longed for their own business. Cindy wanted to capitalize on her knowledge of Asian foods, and soon she had plans for an egg roll manufacturing business. But there was a hitch: they needed $30,000 to buy their custom manufacturing machinery.

Such a small sum, the couple were advised, was beneath what a bank would lend. So instead they were referred to Seattle's Cascadia Revolving Fund, a community development lender.

Cascadia lent the money in May of 1991, and Cindy and Tom spent the next year learning the business, filling small orders, and expanding the product line. When they met a food broker who wanted to put their products in supermarkets around the country, sales took off, and are now running at $500,000 annually, according to general manager Lynette Hoffman.

The company is profitable and Cindy and Tom have demonstrated that the American dream of seizing opportunity to create a better lifestyle is still alive and vibrant. But the real bottom line? Fifteen jobs. Fifteen more people working, because Cindy and Tom had an idea, and because Cascadia displayed confidence in their ability to pull it off. When you consider the total economic impact the company, called Cindy Le's House of Egg Rolls, has had on Seattle, the initial $30,000 loan has been paid back many times over.

What You Can Do

Advocate business lending in your community. Banks are community institutions. Sometimes they forget, or lapse into unresponsiveness. You can easily shake them loose. Here are three ways.

- Ask to review your bank's "CRA file." Don't feel squeamish about asking; the file is there for you to look at. CRA stands for Community Reinvestment Act, a law passed in 1978 to encourage banks to make loans in their communities and to assist in development and redevelopment efforts. Look at the file objectively. Does your bank have a record of investing in the community? If not, express your concern to the manager or president. Bank applications for branch expansion are tied to their community reinvestment record, and the hint of a poor one may jolt them into action.

- Ask your community bank to become a Small Business Administration lender. The SBA is a federal program that, among other things, provides lenders a 90 percent guarantee on loans they make. The problem is, the SBA reports, only larger banks tend to participate in the program. "We need the smaller banks to get involved in the program," says Jack Cleek, public information officer for the SBA's Atlantic region, "because they are much closer to the kinds of loans where we can make a real difference in lending and job creation."

  SBA loans work, too. Jiffy Lube International, Apple Computer, Federal Express, and Compaq Computers all received SBA-guaranteed loans during their formative stages. Look at them go now.

- Offer to guarantee a loan. Banks usually want a personal guarantee on most loans. Generally speaking, though, they don't care whose guarantee it is. If you're in a position to do so, tell your bank president or manager that you would be willing to guarantee a loan or part of a loan for a worthwhile community project. That will really make his or her ears perk up, and maybe make a loan happen.

Even if you can't guarantee a loan, you can still pitch in by making a deposit in a Community Development Loan Fund. In some cases your deposit can be as little as $100. These are private, not-for-profit groups staffed by community and business leaders and funded by churches, private citizens, and, in some cases, other banks, to make small, community-based loans that banks are generally not able to do. Your investment in such a fund will earn you the prevailing market interest rate, but your deposit is not insured. Take comfort in the fact, though, that community funds have good track records. Nationally, the forty-one groups that are members of the National Association of Community Development Loan Funds have experienced losses of less than $1 million on loans of more than $106 million, a record that many banks would envy. In the process, these community funds have created more than 6,000 jobs here in America!

To find out about the fund nearest you, call the National Association of Community Development Loan Funds in Philadelphia. The number is 215-923-4754.

People Who Save American Jobs, and How You Can Too

44

One Man Makes a Difference

*They called him provincial, shortsighted and
out of touch. But Bill Lynott is educating
thousands to buy American.*

OVERVIEW

A split-level suburban house hardly seems the kind of place
where American jobs are being saved. But from his home in
Abington, Pennsylvania, Bill Lynott passionately works to teach
consumers, for free, about the vast array of quality American-
made products now on the market.

Lynott is president of the Buy America Foundation, a nonprofit group he founded after retiring from a career with Sears,
Roebuck and Co. Lynott has lived long enough to see how
America's industrial base has deteriorated, and he is adamant
about doing something to save it. He's not an extremist. Behind
his desk sits a Sony television, his office uses both American
and Japanese computer equipment. But he is a realist. And in
Lynott's view of reality, America is losing an economic war of
titanic proportions. By not buying our own products, he feels,
we have become our own worst enemies. "My feeling is simply
this," begins Lynott. "Not everyone can earn a living in the
service sector. The real source of economic wealth in a country
is adding value through manufacturing. But our manufacturing
base has eroded to such a degree that it's no wonder so many
Americans are out of work."

Lynott's primary weapon in reversing the backslide is a
quarterly newsletter that his group publishes and sends free to
anyone who requests it. The *Buy America Newsletter* profiles

American-made products and companies and exposes those companies and institutions that only pretend to be in support of American workers and products.

Lest you think no one is interested in Lynott's message, consider the 10,000 issues he sends out each printing. And the organization, which was started on a shoestring, is self-supporting, completely dependent on modest donations from members and newsletter recipients.

In recent issues, the *Buy America Newsletter* offered kudos to:

• Carolyn Collins Caviar, which comes from the Midwest and has received rave reviews from food critics. The American caviar sells for four to ten times less than the imported stuff.

• Cooper Tires & Rubber Co., which makes all its tires right in the United States. Moderately priced, the tires come in sizes to fit all makes and models of automobiles.

• Tandy Corporation (parent of Radio Shack), which recently became the first U.S. computer company to export computers to Japan.

• American Tourister, which recently brought its manufacturing back to the United States from Asia.

By the same token, the newsletter gored:

• The Pennsylvania State Lottery, which recently handed out 25,000 promotional baseball caps that read "Buy American." They were made in China.

• A Japanese government official who termed the "Buy American" movement merely "a lot of talk."

• Joseph Gorman, CEO of TRW, a major supplier to Detroit's Big Three. Gorman insisted that his top managers try a Lexus, which is made by Toyota. To make sure they complied, he arranged to lease thirty of the cars.

What You Can Do

Write the Buy America Foundation and ask to be placed on its mailing list.

Buy America Foundation
P. O. Box 82

Abington, Pennsylvania 19001
215-886-3646

And make a donation. The Foundation is completely independent. There's no big-business money behind it. Only Lynott, his supporters, and friends. He's doing good work, and deserves our support.

Get others to order the newsletter. If your company has a newsletter, if your church or civic association publishes printed material, mention it and tell readers how to order it! After all, it's free and loaded with valuable consumer information.

Use the newsletter to help build your own personal library of books vital to understanding the new world economic order. The newsletter frequently reviews new books and articles about the changing global economy. The better we understand the challenges before us, the better are our chances of reclaiming lost economic ground.

Note

You don't think the Japanese are concerned about the Buy America movement? Well, last November, *Nikkei News*, one of Japan's leading business newspapers, dispatched its Detroit bureau chief to Bill Lynott's home for an interview. Why would the Japanese want to know about a retiree working out of his home, half a world away? Because the Japanese are uniquely sensitive to any information that could limit their ability to dominate world markets. The Japanese business press is closely monitoring the Buy America movement in this country, and reporting on it daily.

45

People Who Put Others to Work

Not everyone is cut out to be an entrepreneur. But if you have the inclination, determination, and skill to start a business, now is the time to take the plunge and put people to work.

OVERVIEW

Small business has become the engine of new job creation in this country. As the IBMs, Du Ponts, and Exxons of the world continue to shed layers of management and banish people to the unemployment line, small businesses, those with fewer than 500 employees, quietly continue to create the lion's share of jobs and opportunities for American workers.

Not everybody who starts a business is your prototypical entrepreneur: the fly-by-the-seat-of-the-pants risk-taker who gambles everything to strike it big. On the contrary, many of today's successful entrepreneurs are people who have specialized talents or knowledge and want to create a better life for themselves and their employees.

Consider three quick case studies:

- George Bird never imagined he would own a business with seventy people working for him. A lifelong corporate executive, he was comfortable and secure working for a major pharmaceutical company. But when the 1980s rolled around and his employer started playing the merger and acquisition game, Bird lost confidence in a company that became more interested in making deals than in making products.

182

When the company decided to slash the division that Bird managed and told him to lay off all of its employees, Bird dutifully obliged. But then he made his move. By securing bank and investor financing—including a loan from his former employer—he raised the money to buy a product line from the division his company had closed. Along with colleague Michele LeGear, Bird launched Gen Trak, a Plymouth Meeting, Pennsylvania, manufacturer of blood typing reagents. From a modest beginning of eleven employees, Gen Trak has emerged into a game player in its industry with sales of $8 million and seventy employees in 1992. The company is currently readying new DNA testing technology that could transform the business into a $70 million-a-year company by 1993.

• Shelly Spiegel was a Washington, D.C. attorney who simply didn't want to spend her life playing the adversarial role of a lawyer. When her younger brother asked her to help him find a college to attend, Spiegel searched long and hard. Her conclusion: there had to be a better way for high school seniors to investigate the colleges of their choice.

From that experience, Spiegel started Search By Video, a marketing service that distributes colleges' promotional videotapes to high school students. It's a big help to students who don't have the money to visit ten or twelve schools before narrowing the field of candidates. For about $5 a school, students call Search By Video and the company sends them a single cassette with videos from their requested schools.

The business employs order takers and salespeople, as well as young workers to pack and ship orders. Spiegel currently has a staff of twenty-nine, many of whom are in college and use the money to pay tuition and to buy books.

Without the company, some of the employees' education would be at risk. "With the high cost of college, most of our employees really need money, and they work hard for their salary," says Spiegel. "It's the type of business that supports the hopes and dreams of young kids who want to get ahead."

• Kevin Abt was a hotshot corporate executive with U.S. Sprint, pulling down six figures for launching new products. After he and his wife, Susan, had a child in 1987, they could no longer go out to dinner on moment's notice. Domino's Pizza was their only alternative—until Abt came up with an idea. Why not develop a service that would deliver food from twelve to fifteen restaurants to the doorsteps of homes and businesses?

Abt quit his job and started Takeout Taxi. His former colleagues laughed when they saw him playing delivery boy around his hometown of Herndon, Virginia. And Abt made plenty of early mistakes, losing nearly $250,000 before figuring out how to operate the business profitably.

But he stuck to his dreams and in 1991 began franchising the business. Today, Takeout Taxi franchises operate in fifty-five cities throughout the country. Abt has personally put fifty entrepreneurs in business, many of whom either lost their jobs or feared losing them during the recession of the early 1990s. The ripple effect of his business? Network-wide, Takeout Taxi employs more than 2,500 Americans.

Ironically, Abt is now often approached by the very U.S. Sprint executives who laughed at him. Many are looking for work.

Starting a business is a high-risk proposition. But if that's your dream, now might be the time to pursue it. During a slower economy, rents, supplies, and labor often come cheap. If you get in now and lock in low prices, you stand to gain when the economy heats up and prices and demand increase.

Sources

The United States Small Business Administration has a number of programs and publications designed to help entrepreneurs and small-business people. For a list of SBA publications on starting and managing a small business, write to:

Small Business Directory
P.O. Box 1000
Fort Worth, Texas 76119
800-U-ASK-SBA.

You will be put in touch with the SBA office nearest you.

The SBA's Service Corps of Retired Executives (SCORE) and the Active Corps of Executives (ACE) are volunteer business development programs that link the talents of veteran businesspeople with fledgling entrepreneurs. You can learn more about them through your local SBA office or see page 200 for an address and phone number.

You also might want to check out the following books: *Growing a Business*, by Paul Hawken, describes the experiences and theories of the cofounder of the Smith & Hawken catalog. It's both motivational and useful for learning how to do business in the 1990s. (*Growing a Business*, Fireside, Simon & Schuster.)

The Popcorn Report, by Faith Popcorn, identifies the hot trends for the 1990s and beyond. Many new entrepreneurs have used Popcorn's advice to position their own businesses. (*The Popcorn Report*, Bantam Doubleday Dell Publishing Group.)

Magazines that report on small business include:

Entrepreneur. Call 800-274-6229 to order.

Success. Call 800-234-7324 or 212-951-9500 to order.

INC Magazine. Call 800-234-0999 to order.

Nation's Business. Call 800-727-5869 to order.

Other organizations to consider:

Each industry has a trade association where you can find statistics on the size and future of that field. To find the association that represents your industry, check the Encyclopedia of Associations, available at the reference section of most libraries.

In addition, many cities have entrepreneurial groups that meet to share ideas and discuss small-business issues.

How Education Can Save American Jobs

46

No Train, No Gain

*Constant training is the key to safeguarding your job
in the decades to come.*

OVERVIEW

It used to be your career lasted a lifetime. If you entered the
work force as an engineer, you left as an engineer some forty
years later. Americans were career salespeople, laborers, managers, or marketers. They acquired one set of skills and honed
them finely while working themselves up the ladder of success.

All that has ended. Today, the average American changes
careers six times before retirement. Engineers become industrial
salespeople. Managers transform themselves into consultants. A
teacher becomes an entrepreneur. Nurses go on to become
physicians or researchers or public health administrators.

There is no standing still in the job market of today and
tomorrow. The market for ideas, products, skills, and knowledge changes so quickly that entire industries are being born
overnight or tossed aside in the wake of new discoveries and
new global demands.

You can't afford to be tossed aside with these changes. To stay
ahead, Americans need to become more fluid, less tied to a
single career, company, or even set of skills. The successful
American worker in the year 2000 will have a number of
careers—maybe four or five—during his or her lifetime. And
education, the linchpin of economic endeavor, will become a
lifelong pursuit of most workers.

What You Can Do

Retrain yourself. Never stop learning. Take courses in computers, bookkeeping, sales, administration, motivation, business writing, and/or communications. Be on the lookout for hot new areas of opportunity, such as computer programming or servicing, or health care administration. Then take courses to learn and master the skills needed to move into these new technologies, jobs, or industries.

A Brief Case Study

Edward Cavanagh survived one of the largest corporate cutbacks in the history of America, and he credits ongoing education for helping him keep his job while those around him were losing theirs.

An electrical engineer by training, Cavanagh had no trouble finding a good job after graduating from Manhattan College with a bachelor's of science in 1980. He was doing what he loved—designing large mainframe computers for one of the industry's leaders (whom he asked not to name).

In the old order of work, Cavanagh would have been set for life. But when the mid-1980s rolled around and his company merged with another larger computer firm, Cavanagh watched as jobs and divisions were slashed to pay off debt. When all was said and done, more than 60,000 employees had lost their jobs.

Not Cavanagh. He realized early on in the shake-up that to keep his job he had to become more valuable to the corporation.

To accomplish that, he enrolled in night school and slowly earned an MBA, thanks to his employer's tuition reimbursement plan, one of the few benefits the company didn't cut. The courses complemented his technical knowledge by exposing him to management and marketing for the first time.

He then took advantage of in-house programs the company offered—everything from seminars about teamwork to workshops on productivity and efficiency.

Even after the company had cut all the fat and started excising the muscle, Cavanagh escaped the knife. "I had too much knowledge that the company needed, knowledge that never would have been there if I stopped my education after earning a bachelor's degree."

Cavanagh continues to learn. He's still taking courses, and plans to for the duration of his career.

"American computer workers are the best in the world," says Cavanagh. "But the only way we're going to get the chance to prove it is to keep pushing ourselves to learn as much as we can."

A HOW-TO APPROACH TO RETRAINING YOURSELF

• Start with your employer. Does it have a tuition reimbursement plan? If so, use it to offset the cost of education. If not, go to your employer and ask what skills it will need now and in the future. Tell the company you can save it money by acquiring those skills and putting them to work for the business. After all, you know the business. If your employer could help you finance night school or part-time vocational training, you could provide the skills it needs more efficiently than could a newly hired employee, who wouldn't know the company's policies or procedures.

• If you are out of work because of foreign competition, contact local community colleges and inquire about the Trade Regulations Act, which helps Americans who have lost their jobs due to foreign competition learn new skills. The Act provides for up to two years of training and unemployment compensation. Community colleges are conducting most of this training and can provide you with applications.

• For those of you who need basic reading and writing skills, contact your local Literacy Council Chapter (in the blue pages of your telephone book) or local library. One or both of these sources can put you in touch with volunteers who can work with you on a one-to-one basis to develop reading and writing skills.

192 / How Education Can Save American Jobs

• If you are a veteran, contact your local Veterans Administration to find out what educational and counseling benefits you are entitled to receive.

• Union member? Many unions sponsor retraining programs free to their members. Find out what you are entitled to.

• Attend night school. Local high schools and community colleges often sponsor basic computer and other courses for as little as $100 a semester.

The Skills Needed to Succeed in the Year 2000

1. Typing. Sounds elementary, but you can't work a computer without working a keyboard. Fingers often do the thinking and decision making in the world of information and communication.

2. Basic computer skills. Sure you've heard it before, but according to the Department of Census, only 28 percent of Americans eighteen and older use computers at work or home, but 46 percent of those ages three to seventeen now use them on a daily basis. The computer age is upon us, and those coming up in the workforce already know it. If you don't know how to use a computer, you better start learning fast.

3. Languages. Just about any. The world is getting smaller and smaller. Everyone from telephone operators to factory supervisors will need to speak additional languages if they want to communicate with workers, owners, and customers in far-off lands.

4. Writing and speaking. In the age of information, communication is king. Workers who can articulate through the written and spoken word will always have jobs.

5. Salesmanship. Corporations are slicing layers of management to, in their words, "get closer to consumers." That's just corporate-speak for improving sales and marketing in every level of their organizations. More than ever, companies want employees who know how to get results, and in business, results means sales. The key phrase in many businesses today is, "Everybody sells."

6. Initiative. For too many years, American workers were simply drones who responded to what bosses told them. But today, companies need everyone to take initiative in order to increase productivity. In the world of tomorrow, bosses will look to employees for answers on how to cut costs and enhance productivity. Those who can't respond won't be around.

7. Entrepreneurship. It used to be only management that worried about cutting costs, increasing returns, and improving the bottom line. But in the new workplace, employees will be given more responsibility for making money. Those employees who understand how to read a profit-and-loss statement or write and execute a business plan will be the ones most cherished and rewarded.

47

Putting Education to the Test

American children must learn better if they are
to fill the high-tech jobs of tomorrow.

OVERVIEW

Why aren't more Americans claiming the high-pay, high-tech jobs of the new global economy? They don't have the skills. Our educational system is failing us. When it comes to learning—especially when it comes to learning critical math and science skills—American children aren't keeping pace with students from around the world.

Americans enter the work force with inferior skills that cause employers to look elsewhere when building plants and factories that generate tomorrow's jobs. Where are the jobs going? Try Ireland, India, Indonesia, the Philippines, and other areas throughout the world that offer pockets of highly skilled, highly motivated workers. Shockingly, these countries are doing a better job of educating their young than the United States, which spends more on education than any other country in the world.

America's education system still revolves around nineteenth century agrarian society, when school days ended early so children could milk cows and summer breaks were long so children could help in the fields.

Why aren't educators working to correct the problems? Many American teachers still refuse to acknowledge the shortcomings. They claim that it's impossible to compare America's education system to others in the world. "It's like comparing a basketball team to a football team," argues an American teacher who spent time teaching in Japan. "How do we identify superior teaching?" she questions. Simple: when American children score lower than children in Slovenia in math and science, then something is wrong and needs to be righted.

Facts and Figures

- According to education experts, by the time Japanese teen-agers finish the twelfth grade they have the equivalent of three or four more years of education than U.S. high school graduates.
- Nine out of ten Japanese receive high school diplomas. In the United States, nearly 25 percent of all teenagers drop out, providing a steady flow of workers qualified only to flip hamburgers or mow lawns.
- American schools sit empty for nearly half of each year. While the Japanese spend 240 days a year in school, Ameri-can children attend only 180 days. This hiatus idles our children, allowing them to forget about education during the summer months while other children around the world are using this time to learn the skills they'll need to win future jobs.
- In a survey by the Economic Development Administration, only 12 percent of employers felt that U.S. high school graduates wrote well and only 22 percent believed that they had satisfactory math skills.
- In Europe and Japan teachers are afforded the same status and pay as engineers and other professionals. Few of these teachers study "education," but instead are qualified ex-perts in their areas of expertise.

What You Can Do

Don't waste time waiting for government or educators to improve our school systems. Change in public education is likely to come slowly, if at all. American parents must take it upon themselves to help their children learn the skills necessary to compete in tomorrow's job market.

Sponsor your own education co-op. Teachers are inexpensive. Substitute teachers earn on average $80 a day in most school systems in this country. You and three or four other families can rent a substitute teacher for less than $50 (that's about $12.50 each) for a Saturday morning's worth of tutoring.

How to find the right teacher. Call the business office of your local school district. If you don't think your school district is top-notch, call the business office of a school district that comes highly recommended. Ask for the chair of the science, math, or reading department to recommend a substitute to tutor your children. Ask which substitute teachers do the best job of instructing children. Get their names and telephone numbers.

Contract with the teacher. Work out a pay schedule with the teacher. Contract for as many weeks as possible. Conduct the sessions at one of the families' homes or request permission from the school to let you use its facilities on Saturday. Attend the co-op classes with your children to keep track of what they are learning.

Work closely with your children's regular teachers. Tell your children's regular teachers about your co-op. Ask them to provide weekly updates on what lessons were covered so the co-op can reinforce what was learned.

Make the co-op special. One problem with American education is that it relies on structured lectures to teach children. Your co-op can be free-flowing, with hands-on learning sessions. For instance, you can conduct a half-day experiment or you can bring in guest speakers from local engineering firms or other businesses skilled in math and science. Many businesses are anxious to contribute to local education in any way possible. Create a partnership with high-tech or scientific businesses to make real-world learning a part of your co-op. Don't overlook local colleges or even retired college professors as sources for guest teachers and instructors.

Attend local school board meetings and submit ideas to your state representatives in the National Education Associa-

tion. Most changes in school curricula are mandated by local school boards, which are made up of elected officials. Attend the regular meetings. Most school boards are required to set aside time on their agendas for public response and opinion. Take advantage of this time. Bring friends and fellow parents to these meetings. Public pressure makes a difference to these elected officials.

48

Doing the Numbers

The jobs of the future will rely on advanced math and science—the very areas in which Americans are lacking.

OVERVIEW

At a Hewlett-Packard computer plant in Guadalajara, half the employees have advanced degrees. At a General Electric light bulb plant in Hungary, the engineering talent surpasses that in America. At an industrial plant in the former East Germany, the engineering skills inherited by its new American owner dazzle company management.

There was a time when the only work going overseas was low-paying, manual labor that Americans did not want to perform. That was then. Today, knowledge and technology flow easily across international borders. The jobs leaving America are no longer of the menial, low-paying, sweatshop variety. Instead, the new global work force is grabbing skill-intensive, science-and-math-dependent jobs that Americans once held.

It's all part of a worldwide push in education and training, and it's aimed at landing jobs for graduates of such schools as Trinity College in Dublin or Indian Institute of Science in Bangalore, India. You might not have heard of these colleges, but corporate recruiters and the managers who decide where to place businesses have. These universities produce some of the top minds in science and math, who are winning jobs at Americans' expense. But don't blame them. Blame us.

Our Fall From Scientific Grace

While America still produces some of the top researchers and scientists in the world, this may not be our destiny in the future. Math and science education is not trickling down to the masses. America's young people labor under the misconception that math is boring, that science is unrelated to their world. The American education system does a spotty job of instilling the math and science skills our children need to compete with their counterparts in Hungary, Mexico, Ireland, and the emerging unified Germany. When *U.S. News & World Report* asked twenty-two experts in comparative education to rate how well industrial nations did in teaching their children, the United States scored behind Japan, the former Soviet Union, Germany, and France in science and mathematics. Our fall in math and science is seen in just about every measure. Consider the following:

- Japan, with only half the population, produces 10 percent more engineers than the United States.
- In the former Soviet Union, students study physics and algebra for five years, chemistry and biology for four, and calculus for two. The majority of American teenagers never take a single physics or chemistry class, and only 6 percent study calculus.
- On an International Science Test, eighteen-year-old American students answered fewer questions correctly than students in many other tested countries, including Australia, Canada, Finland, Great Britain, Hong Kong, Hungary, Italy, Japan, Norway, Poland, Singapore, and Sweden.
- A study conducted by the Educational Testing Service found a negative relationship in about half the tested countries between the amount of television watched and mathematical performance. American students are world-class television watchers, spending from ages six to eighteen, about 15,000 hours watching TV. That's about 2,000 hours more than they spend in school.

What You Can Do

Americans need to do more to provide young people with an understanding and appreciation of math and science. We need to expose our children to the power and potential of technology and technical learning earlier in their lives, and then make sure they absorb these critical lessons throughout their education.

Parents have to stop accepting schools' mediocre performance in teaching math and science, and must take an active role in advancing these critical skills.

Become an involved parent. Form a science and math support group with other parents in your child's classes. Meet informally with parents and teachers on-site at schools to map out strategies for upgrading math and science lessons. Here's how:

- Encourage teachers to include outside researchers and scientists in the education of your children. Have parents participate by bringing their real-world knowledge of science or math into the classroom.
- Form working partnerships with area businesses engaged in scientific pursuits. Ask them to supply speakers, equipment, demonstrations, etc.
- Find computers for your schools. Go to local businesses and ask them to donate unused computer equipment to your schools.
- Start a science videotape library. Ask each parent to purchase an educational videotape about science or math. Topics can range from dinosaurs to volcanoes, aerodynamics to engineering. Make the videos part of a special pool you share with other parents in your coffee-klatch group.
- Do not accept excuses. Slashed budgets and teacher inertia are no excuses for accepting mediocrity in the classroom.

Take Carolyn Staudt, for instance. Staudt teaches science subjects at Copley High School in Copley, Ohio.

With no school funding and only her own energy and creativity, Staudt has twice transformed the front lawn of her high school into Moonbase Copley, a 4,000-square-foot learning center that brings science to life for her teenage students.

The experimental learning station, which is built from a polyurethane skin stretched over a plastic framework, consisted of one 50-foot geodesic dome connected spiderlike to nine smaller offshoot pods. Inside, Staudt's students learn for themselves what life would be like in a similar world on a lunar outpost.

The key to Staudt's success? She involves students and parents. Companies and corporations donate materials. NASA even made a contribution—actual moon rocks for the students to study.

The lesson: support is out there for educational excellence in science and math. But greatness won't be achieved unless parents get involved.

Teach your children at home. Our own government, through the Department of Education, warns parents not to assume that their children are learning science at school. They urge parents to do whatever they can at home.

- Take young children to ponds and nature areas to show them biology in action.
- Buy a home computer and subscribe to Prodigy, CompuServe, or any other on-line computer service that would allow children to tap into information.
- Limit television watching to ten hours a week. Direct your children to television shows and videos that report on biology, medicine, or physics, such as "Nova," "National Geographic," and "Newton's Apple."
- Allow your young children to shop and cook alongside you. Familiarize them with prices, measures, and weights.
- Go to the library and steer your children toward books on science and/or mathematics.

Sources

Library Video of Bala-Cynwyd, Pennsylvania, a videotape distribution company, recommends the following videos to teach those from age two to eighteen about science:

1. *Earth at Risk* environmental series, by Schlessinger Video Productions.

2. *Miracle of Life,* an Emmy Award-winning Nova video that tracks the evolution of the fetus.

3. *National Geographic* series, an award-winning thirty-volume set that addresses a wide range of scientific topics.

4. *Life on Earth*, science at its most interesting; narrated by David Attenborough.

5. *Cosmos*, the fascinating science series hosted by Carl Sagan.

49

Trading Places

Apprenticeship programs are the keys to developing the highly skilled workers we need to compete.

OVERVIEW

What makes Germany a worldwide industrial powerhouse? Its system of youth apprenticeships encourages vocation-minded youngsters to study and train for the kinds of jobs its economy needs. Two-thirds of all Germans between the ages of sixteen and nineteen take part in apprenticeships. Here in the United States, it's a different story: only about 300,000 people are in apprenticeship programs, and their average age is twenty-seven.

What does this mean? It means that less than 1 percent of the American labor force is exposed to the technical training that American managers need to keep their factories and businesses running at peak performance.

Instead, our youth are funneled into college, even though many of them would be better suited to learn a high-demand skill, and even though many of them never graduate. Those who do graduate often don't have the real-world skills needed to make something the world wants.

We can no longer afford this loss of productivity. America's businesses cannot and America's young people cannot. It's time to take them under our wing, give them a skill, and then let them fly.

A Brief Case Study

When Paul Batowski, labor relations manager for Textron, a manufacturer of small-aircraft engines, surveyed the factory floor, he saw a problem. A big problem. "The average age in there is fifty-five years old. In six years, seven years, I don't have anybody." Not anyone, he means, with the skills the company requires to stay on top of its intensely competitive industry.

When he began looking for tool designers in 1989, Batowski placed ads in newspapers and magazines, and as a last-ditch effort even broadcast the opening, and its starting salary of $30,000, on local television stations. What did he get? Nothing.

So Textron and six other firms took advantage of a state-sponsored youth apprenticeship program. The students in the program, who spend two days a week on-site and three in class, get paid. The company, however, makes a far larger investment in the time their workers spend with the apprentices, to make sure these young people learn the skills needed to carry on the firm's tradition. The program lasts two years, with an option for two more years in combination with training at a local college.

One of the program's catches, Timothy McKee, would by many benchmarks not have seemed like much of a catch at all. The eighteen-year-old high school junior missed a third of his 180 school days in 1991. He was flunking out. McKee parroted the often-heard, and sometimes not inaccurate, teenage cry that goes: "I saw no practical use for what they were teaching us."

But when McKee (along with five other apprentices) found himself next to machinists who were operating sophisticated equipment pumping out precision metal alloy parts, some worth $20,000 each, cutting classes became a thing of the past. And after apprentices helped out in the metrology department, where the intricate gauges manufactured at the plant are measured for accuracy up to twenty-millionths of an inch, teachers reported a renewed interest in algebra, geometry, and trigonometry.

"In four years," said Batowski, "there's no question these students will be ready to come to work as full-time employees, and I'm certain there will be a long line of potential employers for them."

What You Can Do

Start a youth apprenticeship program where you work. In almost every work environment, apprentices can be utilized. For example, Project ProTech in Boston provides high school students part-time working and learning opportunities in area hospitals. If you are an employee, talk to the president of your company or the director of personnel about youth apprenticeships. Here are some key points to make sure they understand:

- Youth apprenticeships can be an inexpensive source of enthusiastic labor.

- Youth apprenticeships are the most effective method to ensure that the company develops a deep well of skilled talent to draw from.

- Youth apprenticeships are, in some cases, partially funded by the state and federal government.

- Youth apprenticeships enhance the skill base of the local, regional, and national work force.

Here are some things you can offer to do for your employer to help get the program going:

- Develop a list of coworkers who have expressed their willingness to teach apprentices their skills.
- Write a plan for integrating apprentices into your company's current operational work flow.
- Develop a list of duties that you believe an apprentice could perform effectively that are either not done now or not done well.
- Contact companies that utilize youth apprenticeship programs and record some of their suggestions for a successful launch.
- Develop a list of the most critical skills that your company needs in its new employees.

The Next Step

The organizations listed below can give you more information on how to get a youth apprenticeship program going.

The U.S. Department of Labor can tell you about the school-to-work programs that it currently funds. Write to the Employment and Training Administration, Office of Work-Based Learning, U.S. Department of Labor, 200 Constitution Avenue NW, Washington, D.C. 20213.

The U.S. Department of Education will fill you in on the opportunities provided by the Tech-Prep Education Program, established by the Carl D. Perkins Vocational and Applied Technology Education Act of 1990. Write the Office of Vocational and Adult Education, U.S. Department of Education, 400 Maryland Avenue SW, Washington, D.C. 20202.

The American Association of Community Colleges has some of the most up-to-date information on "tech-prep" efforts, and will share it with you. Write AACC, One DuPont Circle NW, Suite 410, Washington, D.C. 20036.

Jobs for the Future, a nonprofit group in Cambridge, Massachusetts, whose goal is to improve work-force quality in the United States, can assist with program design, implementation, curriculum development, and evaluation. Write to Richard Kazis, Vice President of Policy and Research, Jobs for the Future, 1815 Massachusetts Avenue, Cambridge, Massachusetts 02140.

Sounds all too familiar, we know, but it's true—for valuable information on youth apprenticeships, a good place to start is your state department of labor or education. In addition, many states have bureaus of apprenticeship training. If your state has one, ask if it also administers any youth programs.

A Word to the Wise

Unions and union members are often sensitive about youth apprenticeships. Sometimes they are viewed as management's attempt to bring in inexpensive labor. If you initiate an apprenticeship program, take pains to explain your goals and objectives to the union. And be sure to remind it that more workers means more potential members for the union, too.

50

Encourage Your Children to Work

When children work today, it helps give America the human resources needed to create jobs in the year 2000.

OVERVIEW

The numbers from the Bureau of Labor Statistics are clear. Eighty-six percent of the jobs requiring professional, technical, or managerial skills are expanding, while 93 percent of blue-collar jobs are contracting. And a projection to the year 2000 shows that occupations requiring a high school diploma will rise by 17 percent and those for dropouts just 15 percent. In short, the average amount of schooling required at the turn of the century will go way up.

Are we ready? In a word, no, because America is afflicted with an appalling dropout rate. Every day some 3,800 American teens drop out of school. Nationally, the rate is approaching 30 percent. In large cities, it's sometimes as high as 60 percent.

One of the primary reasons for this dropout rate is that teens do not see a clear connection between their class work and what they will need to succeed in a job or career. Why struggle with physics when you don't know what you will ever use it for? Or math? Or English? Or a foreign language? Why indeed, when the world of work and the world of school are almost entirely separate?

The cure is simple. Get teens working. According to Jeffrey Newman, executive director of the National Child Labor Committee (NCLC) in New York City, "Work experience for most kids is a very good idea. It provides a glimpse into the real social world young people are moving toward and offers them a sense of identity and importance."

When teens work, two favorable results occur. One, the overall productivity and wealth of the economy are increased. Two, it develops the work ethic and the interest in education that will allow America to compete in the global economy now upon us.

What You Can Do

Get your children working. Not all the time; maybe during the summers, or maybe a day on weekends. And not necessarily for the money. Get them working for the experience, for the technical skills, for the exposure, and for the connection between what happens in the classroom and what happens in the world of work. Here are four things your can do to help:

- Set your children up in their own businesses. Don't force your children and don't do the work for them, but be an enabler. Buy the leashes for a dog-walking business, or the extra phone line for a wake-up service, or the tools for a lawn care business, or the pushcart for a food service business.
- Enroll your child in Junior Achievement programs through their school. Thanks to support from some 24,000 businesses, there is no cost to you or the school. Under the supervision of experienced business people, your children can start their own small company during after-school hours. If your school does not have a Junior Achievement program, call the organization's headquarters to inquire about getting one started. Call or write: Junior Achievement, One Education Way, Colorado Springs, Colorado 80906, 719-540-8000.
- Encourage your child to take a fast-food job. According to the NCLC's Newman, "Fast-food jobs are not dead-end jobs. They can be wonderful. A 15- or 16-year-old at a Wendy's is growing in very important ways and learning what he or she can't in school." In addition, your child will learn just how difficult it is to earn a living in today's world.

• Encourage large corporations near where you live to enter into partnerships with area schools. Many large companies take an active role in their area school system, because it supplies their most fundamental and important resource: employees. The Conference Board, a New York City-based public policy and research institute, applauded this innovative partnership in the Houston metropolitan area:

Tenneco works closely with Jefferson Davis High School. Sixty employee volunteers work with the school, and an additional 107 workers as mentors to students. In addition, the company has created 130 summer jobs for students, which include a week at a leadership camp, and has sent some thirty area principals to seminars at Texas A&M and Harvard University.

How do you get one of these programs going? Write to the president of a medium to large business in your area and ask him or her to be a partner with a nearby school. Or meet with your child's high school principal and ask what you can do to help initiate a partnership program.